Pat m.

## Third Edition, 1990

This edition includes extensive rewriting and updating. Fresh material includes a new economic order, family planning, Islamic education, environment and development.

The titles and positions describing those who speak in the book are, for most part, as held by them at the time the statements were made.

# THE MUSLIM MIND

# THE MUSLIM MIND
## *by Charis Waddy*

*Bismillāh al-raḥmān al-raḥīm:*
"In the Name of God, Most Gracious, Most Merciful"

NEW AMSTERDAM
*New York*

This third edition published in the United States of America in 1990 by
    New Amsterdam Books
    171 Madison Avenue
    New York, NY 10016
by arrangement with Grosvenor Books, London.

Originally published by Longman Group Ltd.
First edition 1976.
Second edition 1982.
Copyright © 1976 and 1982 by the Longman Group Ltd.


*The Library of Congress Cataloging-in-Publication Data is available.*

ISBN 1-56131-014-X (paperback)

*This book is printed on acid-free paper.*

Printed in the United States of America.
Third Edition

*This book is respectfully dedicated to*
*His Eminence Dr Muhammad Abdul Halim Mahmud*
*Shaikh al-Azhar*

He writes:

In the name of God, Most Gracious, Most Merciful

I thank the writer for her kind dedication.

She is right to say that Islam is a religion of universal character. The word "Islam" itself signifies clearly that this religion is a world religion, for linguistically a Muslim is one who is sincere in his worship of God.

The Prophet (God's mercy and blessing be upon him) when asked to define Islam said: "It is to submit your heart to God and to harm no one by word or deed." Sincerity towards God and the surrender of the heart to Him are universal principles independent of time and place.

If we examine the concept of Islam linguistically and theologically we find that it is the very same concept as that of the word "faith". For faith means submission to God and full acceptance of what he commands and what he forbids. His orders and prohibitions form the highest morality. And since the concept of Islam is universal, its morality, its legal system and its social order are also of world relevance.

We appreciate the attitude of the authoress, and the motive that has led her to consider Islam in its universal aspect. May God grant her every success.

Al-Azhar

5 Jumada ii 1395
15 June 1975

vii

# Acknowledgements

We are grateful to the following for permission to reproduce copyright material:

The American Friends of the Middle East for an extract from "Focus on Population", a Special Number of *Mid-East: A Middle East-North African Review*, September/October 1968; George Allen & Unwin Ltd and Macmillan Publishing Co. Inc. for an extract from *A Moslem Saint for The Twentieth Century* by Martin Lings ©; George Allen & Unwin Ltd 1961 and State University of New York Press for two extracts by A. J. Arberry and the Charles Strong Memorial Lecture in *Sufi Essays* by Seyyed Hossein Nasr; Blandford Press Ltd for an extract from *Arab Socialism* by Abdel Moghny Said; The Devin-Adair Company for an extract from *The Eternal Message of Muhammad* by Abd-al Rahman Azzam; the author for an extract from *Towards a Unity of Educational Thought in the Muslim World* by Dr Mohammed Fadhel Jamali; F. J. Goulding for an extract from *A Muslim Commentary on the Universal Declaration of Human Rights* by F. J. Goulding; Hutchinson Publishing Group Ltd and the Grove Press Inc. for extracts from *The Autobiography of Malcolm X* by Alex Haley; the *Guardian* for an extract from an article by Mrs Sadat in the *Guardian* 16 March 1974; *Himmat* for an extract from an article by Neerja Choudhury from *Himmat* 4 February 1972; *Milliyet* for an article by Huseyin Uzmez in *Milliyet* 31 December 1975; the author for an extract from *Concept of Man in Islam* by Ali Issa Othman; Scientific Research House for an extract from *Ḥajj, Pilgrimage Form and Essence* by Dr Hassan Hathout; *The Times* for an article "Man of the Future Seen Through Eastern Eyes" by Dr Charis Waddy from *The Times Educational Supplement* 26 September 1968. Reproduced by permission.

Some of the material in this book has already appeared in *Middle East International*.

We regret that we are unable to trace the copyright holders of the following:

An extract from *The Holy Qur'ān* by A. Yusuf Ali, an extract from a review in *Middle East Forum* Vol. XIV No. 3 and an extract from an article by Rajmohan Gandhi in the *Vancouver Sun* September 1958.

For permission to reproduce the following illustrations, the publishers
are indebted to:

Kitabfurusi Esh-Shayar, from *Faza'ilu, Atlas-i Khatt*: pp. 37, 44, 48,
50, 74, 92
Ministry of Information, Iran, from *Bada i al-Khatt al-Arabi*: pp. 68,
81, 117, 157
Musée Nicolas Sursock, from *Art Islamique*: pp. xviii, 1, 23
Metropolitan Museum of Art, New York: p. 18
Oxford University Press, from *Early Muslim Architecture*, by K. A.
C. Creswell: p. 58
Turkish Press: pp. 77, 154
Elek Books, from *Moorish Spain*, by E. Sordo: p. 90
*Nigerian Field*, September 1974, from "A Leather Worker in Zaria
City", by David Heathcote; and *Savanna*, Vol. 3, No. 1, 1974,
from "Aspects of Style in Hausa Embroidery", by David Heathcote:
p. 108
*Aramco World Magazine*: p. 112
University of Chicago Press, from *The Sense of Unity*, by N. Ardalan
and N. Bakhtiyar: pp. 129, 130
Victoria and Albert Museum: pp. 32, 148
Courtesy of the Smithsonian Institution, Freer Gallery of Art, Wash-
ington D.C.: p. 176
*Radio Times* Hulton Picture Library: p. 29

The publishers also wish to thank the Oriental Institute, Oxford, and
the Department of Eastern Art, The Ashmolean Museum, for their
courtesy in allowing the use of material in their care.

# A Note on quotations from the Qur'ān

All passages from the Qur'ān have been checked with the Arabic and with two approved English "interpretations":

> Mohammed Marmaduke Pickthall, *The Meaning of the Glorious Koran, An Explanatory Translation*. Allen and Unwin, 1939, and Mentor Paperback.

> Abdullah Yusuf Ali, *The Holy Qur'ān – Text, Translation and Commentary*, 2 vols. Dar al-Arabia, First Edition Lahore 1934; Islamic Foundation, Leicester, 1975; Amanah Corporation, Brentwood, Maryland USA 1989.

In 1980, another "interpretation" appeared, to mark the opening of the Fifteenth Century of the Hijra: *The Message of the Qur'ān*, translated and explained by Muhammad Asad, *Dar al-Andalus*, Gibraltar, distributors E. J. Brill, 41 Museum Street, London. The massive commentary by Sayyid Abul A'lā Mawdūdī, *Tafhīm al-Qur'ān*, is being published in English by the Islamic Foundation, Leicester. The first volume, *Towards Understanding the Qu'rān* translated and edited by Zafar Ishaq Ansari, appeared in 1988, the second volume in 1989.

In the many passages quoted to me by Muslims, I have usually left the rendering as they gave it, when a slightly different turn of phrase in no way affected the meaning but helped to reach a foreign ear.

The Qur'ān is divided into chapter and verse. Each chapter (*sūra*) has its name, drawn either from the subject matter (*Joseph, Mary, The Pilgrimage*, etc.) or from some word prominent near its beginning (*The Bee, The Star, The Overwhelming Event*, etc.). It is the name and not the number that enables a Muslim to place the verse. Muslim authors often give both, and I have followed this usage.

For the English reader, A. J. Arberry's *The Koran Interpreted* (World Classics, Oxford University Press, 1964) brings most dignity and beauty to the attempt to render both the meaning and something of the poetry of the original. But in this book I have throughout used the work of Muslims.

Hajji Riadh El-Droubie kindly checked the renderings and the references to the Holy Qur'ān. I thank him for this service.

# Contents

# Introduction

Far to the South, where the Australian coast faces towards the Antarctic, and sea winds sweep inland to break defeated on the sun-parched wastes of the interior, there stands a little mosque.

Hemmed in by the busy, thriving streets of modern Adelaide, it comes as a surprise. It represents the southernmost point of advance of that tide of ideas and of men which started to flow out from Mecca some fourteen hundred years ago – a tide that has ebbed and flowed but has never spent its force.

It was the desert that brought those Muslims to Australia a century and more ago. They and their camels opened up the routes into the interior: westwards to Perth across the wide Nullarbor plains, and northwards by the desert trail along which later the railway was laid. They were known indiscriminately as Ghans, wherever they came from, and some did indeed come from Afghanistan. The train that wends its way northward today from Adelaide to Alice Springs and Darwin is still called the Ghan Express.

Camels to ride, to load, to harness: these were part of the history of Australian development. Enthusiasts for this ancient domestic servant of man foresaw a new chapter in its long history. But the Australian pioneers never took too kindly to either the camels or their masters. The use of the camel continued only until another servant was found which could carry its own water and fuel over even longer distances. In the 1920's the lorry outmoded the camel. The camel drivers turned their remaining herds loose to live wild in the interior, and went their way homewards. The camels re-appeared in the news in 1975 when four of their descendants, from the parched deserts of the Northern Territories, formed Australia's official gift to King Khalid of Saudi Arabia on his accession.

For a while the Adelaide mosque seemed outmoded: but not for long. The end of World War II saw a fresh tide of New Australians. One of these, who came from Jugoslavia in 1950, was for years Imam at the mosque the camel drivers built. The weekly congregation comes from many countries. There are students from Malaysia, Indonesia and a number of African countries. There are immigrants from Arab countries, and from Turkey, which in the Seventies sent a large number of families to settle in Australia every year. This is a small group compared with those who gather in other Australian capitals on Fridays or Sundays, with schemes for large mosques and centres: in the

1980's 90,000 Muslims resided in New South Wales alone. These congregations reflect the vigour, the cohesion, the variety, the expansive capacity that can be found wherever Muslims are making a new home, or where new Muslims are finding their place in a world brotherhood.

I have twice approached the Muslim world from this southern angle. First, just after the First World War, when my father took his Australian family to live in Palestine. The fascination and the tension, the hopes and the prejudices of that formative period were deeply etched in a child's mind.

The second time was fifty years and almost a lifetime later. Then I could linger on the way: glimpse Indonesia and Malaysia; savour the glories of Islamic architecture, the masterpieces of Muslim builders in Agra and Isfahan, Cairo and Istanbul.

To come by this route provides a healthy change of approach for the western mind. Stilled are the echoes of Roland's horn in the Pyrenees, and of Turks hammering at Vienna. Old clichés which have been locks on the doors of understanding can be disregarded. Ears can be opened to hear the call to prayer, and hearts to appreciate the wisdom and grace of a life style other than our own.

Every Muslim looks towards Mecca as he prays. Many carry a compass as they travel, to point the direction accurately.

Draw the line to Mecca from that southernmost mosque, and it crosses thousands of miles of Indian and Arabian ocean to reach its destination. It bypasses Sri Lanka, pivot and link between western and eastern Islam. North of the line stretches the whole eastern half of the Muslim crescent: the populous lands of Indonesia, the Malaysian peninsula, Mindanao in the Philippines, India, Pakistan and Bangladesh. For all of these, to turn towards Mecca is to look west. Still further north are the Afghans and Iranians. Beyond them live many millions of Muslims in the Soviet Union and China, some of them descendants of converts made along the ancient silk and spice routes, when in the early days of Islam Muslim traders took their faith with them, as they do today in Africa.

In the Arab heartlands of the followers of the Prophet, over one hundred and sixty million Arabs live in twenty independent countries, from the Taurus to the Indian Ocean, the Atlantic to the Gulf. South of these are the ever-expanding congregations of Africa. Over half the total population of the African continent is Muslim. There are Muslim majorities in Nigeria and Ethiopia, as well as in the Saharan belt: and considerable minorities elsewhere. In Western Europe over six million

Muslims live and work and more than that in Eastern Europe.[1] And still we have not taken note of large communities in the United States; of the Muslims of Indian descent in the West Indies and Surinam; of Syrians in Latin America. Today it would be hard to find a country without its Muslim community, large or small.

The number of those who profess Islam is steadily rising. Population projections based on United Nations estimates made in 1975 indicate that the world total of Muslims by the year 2000 AD will be about 1.4 billion, said the 1985 edition of the *World Muslim Gazetteer*, published by the World Muslim Congress in Karachi.[2] Its estimate of the total in 1975 was 900 million, with Muslim majorities in forty-six independent states. This compares with the figure of 647 million given in the 1964 edition. The rise is in line with the rapid population growth in Asia and Africa generally, including the countries with the largest numbers of Muslims: Indonesia and Bangladesh, India and Pakistan, Nigeria, Turkey and Egypt.

The other large figures given in the Gazetteer concern the Soviet Union and China. Central Asia has always been an area of great influence in the Muslim world. Islam reached the Caucasus in the Seventh Century AD, and spread quickly across Central Asia as far as China. It expanded northward later during the Mongol period. Its cities – Bukhara, Samarkand and others – were famous centres of learning. Russian conquest was followed by the establishment in the 1920's of six Soviet republics in lands traditionally Muslim. Azerbaidzhan south of the Caucasus and between the Black Sea and the Caspian, borders on Iran. The other five make up the Central Asian Region of the USSR: Kazakhstan, Uzbekistan, Turkmenistan, Tadzhikistan, and Kirghiz on the Chinese border. According to the Soviet census of 1959, the population of Muslim origin was then over 30 million. Following the 1979 census it has been estimated as 50 or 55 million. After a long period of isolation and oppression, they are emerging once again on to the world scene.

In China, there are two types of Muslim community. Scattered throughout China are the *Hui*, who owe their origin to merchants and travellers settling in China from the Seventh Century onwards. In North West China, and especially in the province of Xinjiang, there are Central Asian groups who have maintained their ethnic and as well as their religious identity. Numbers given vary widely. *The World Muslim Gazetteer* in 1964 gave the figure of over 50 millions "as a safe assumption". In 1975 it raised this to 93 millions. Official sources continued to quote a much lower figure.[3]

The range of the Muslim world is as wide as the human race, and its peoples are deeply involved in every major problem that confronts our common humanity. The faith they profess is simple. The history to which it has given birth is as rich and complex as any – as high in civilisation and as full of contrasts. On some of its borders it has advanced peacefully: in the Far East, for instance, and still today in Africa. In other border lands there have been centuries of conflict, as in Cyprus and Eritrea.

There have been internal tensions also, the earliest being the division between Sunnis and Shi'is. This dates back to the days of the immediate sucessors of the Prophet, when 'the party of 'Ali' emphasised the importance of Muḥammad's family, especially 'Ali himself and his wife Fatima, daughter of Muḥammad. The subsequent historical tensions have taken many forms, but the basic tenets of the faith – such as Prayer, Fasting, Pilgrimage, and reverence for the Qur'ān – are held by all. Today, about ten per cent of Muslims are Shi'ites, the greatest numbers being in Iran and Iraq. Shi'ism is the official form of Islam in Iran.

Only at the most sixteen per cent of Muslims have Arabic, the language of the Qur'ān, as their mother tongue. Muslims are ruled by a wide variety of governments, from sheikhdoms to republics. Outside countries where they form a majority, millions of Muslims are loyal citizens of almost every modern state.

Among these are the Muslims of India. They form an integral part of its experiment in creating a democratic, secular society where all are meant to be free to contribute out of their own faith and traditions. When partition took place in 1947, they chose to remain in India, as Indians. They still formed the second largest Muslim population in the world, exceeded only by Indonesia, though since surpassed by Pakistan and possibly by China. Pakistan, which came into being with its two wings in 1947, divided into two separate states in 1972, with the formation of Bangladesh. The government of Indonesia, like that of India, is based on secular and democratic principles. In the Arab countries (except Lebanon), in Iran, Pakistan and Bangladesh the governments are officially Muslim.

It is a matter of some importance to understand the values and beliefs of so large and influential a segment of the human race. At the United Nations or at any of the world conferences where men grapple with current problems, almost a quarter of the delegates are likely to have a background of the Muslim faith. The immense oil wealth of some Muslim countries has compelled the rest of us to pay more heed to them, and to realise that there are few problems which can be solved without a greater understanding of the way their minds work.

The chequered history of the past does not make this easy. There are bloodstained pages on both sides of the record, and old wounds still fester. But even at the times when confrontation has been most bitter, there have been voices in both Islam and Christendom giving a truer interpretation of the spirit of both religions. The simplistic view of the Chanson de Roland – *"Chrétiens ont droit, païens ont tort"* – has never been the limit of western thought. At the height of the period of crusading fervour, for example, Peter the Venerable commissioned a translation of the Qur'ān in Latin. When Europe was threatened by the Ottoman invasions, the Swiss scholar Bibliander made sure that the new invention of printing should bring the Qur'ān to the attention of scholars and statesmen. His edition, first published in 1543, is still to be found on the shelves of the great libraries of Europe. His comment was, "The beginning of all these wars, captivities and plagues may be clearly perceived to be in ourselves which are Christian men by name only, not in deeds and living. The same ungracious deeds which we abhor in others, yea or greater mischiefs, are done amongst Christians . . . Neither would Mahumet seem at any hand to be Christ's enemy."[4]

Since his day, western attitudes towards Islam have often been shaped by some dim and biased memory of the Crusades, or nowadays by headlines of political or military activities in Muslim countries. It would be unfair to judge the merit of Christian faith and philosophy by IRA or extreme Protestant action in Ireland, yet that is how Islam is often viewed. Such attitudes have led to dangerous confusions at a policy level. Western statesmen have failed to grasp the fundamental opposition between dialectical materialism and Islam. They have also failed to assess the determination in the Muslim world to provide an alternative to the materialism of both the capitalist and the communist systems. Lack of clarity has led to disastrous misunderstandings, and increased the danger of making the Middle East the cockpit of a world war.

The basic tenets of Islam come alive most simply in what Muslims themselves say. So, in this book, I have set down what has been said to me by Muslims from all over the world. It is not an exhaustive analysis of the Muslim mind, but a collection of material which has illumined that mind for me. It is drawn from dozens of conversations with Muslims, and from books which they have recommended. The book is the fruit of their friendship.

So many people have helped me in compiling it over several years that it is not possible to mention them all here by name. I hope that each and every one of those who have been so generous with their time and their knowledge, with suggestion and criticism, and with hospitality, will recognise in the book itself some token of my gratitude. I would also like to thank the Spalding Trust, which gave me a research grant at the suggestion of the late Professor Arberry.

One of those first consulted said to me, "This is a new approach – finding out what the living authorities think. To enter into another culture and religion should be a mutual enrichment as well as an endeavour to understand. We need humility, and respect for each other. This involves recognising that intelligent, educated men and women can believe things that differ from what I believe myself. You will interview common people as well as learned. The ordinary reader will be more interested in *us* than in other people's ideas about us."[5]

Many of those I talked with are acutely aware of the gap between the ideal and the reality, and of the need to bridge it. One correspondent writes, "A student of Islam will at once realise how different contemporary Muslims are from Islam. Had they been following Islam in the life they lead, I am sure the picture would be quite different. Perhaps much of what there is, is due to the abandonment of Islamic teaching and not to Islam. As the great Nineteenth Century reformer Muhammad Abduh said: 'Islam is concealed from western people by a heavy curtain of Muslims.' "[6]

Any honest Christian must echo this conviction, in regard to our own situation in so-called Christian lands. It should not stop us from seeking to assess the true potential of a great tradition.

"What comes from the lips, reaches the ear. What comes from the heart, reaches the heart." So runs the Arab proverb. It is from heart to heart that the bridges of the future must be built.

Tile: Medina, mosque and tomb of the Prophet
Isnik, Turkey, c. 1660 AD

# PART ONE
## *The Road*

# CHAPTER ONE
## *The Straight Way*

When you want to understand Islam,
where do you go? A learned professor
has said that we must go to the diction-
ary and scholarship, and then to the
mosque. Certainly it is necessary to go
to these places, but going there alone
will be incomplete. Islam is not confined to the mosque – it is a code of
conduct and a guidance for everyday
life. We have to watch the career of a
Muslim who has himself understood
the religion of Islam and who practises
its principles. Without that watching,
the mosque or the textbook will give
us only an incomplete understanding.

The Honourable Justice M. M. Ismail, Madras[1]

Islam's conception of life is often put in terms of a road. A road has a beginning and a destination. The individual is somewhere on the road between birth and death. The human race is on the road too — the road from Creation to Judgment.

The millions now turning their faces to Mecca pray many times a day: "Show us the straight way." "Guide us in the straight path." *Al-Fātiḥa*, the opening chapter (*sūra*) of the Qur'ān with its seven verses, is repeated at each of the five times of prayer.

Whole books have been written on these verses. They are the first to be memorised by children, and they are pondered by statesmen. An ex-Prime Minister, asked what was the inspiration behind his success in recent negotiations, went through the Fātiḥa step by step.

The first volume of one modern "explanatory translation" of the Qur'ān is entirely devoted to this opening chapter. "Let us look at the *Sūrat al-Fātiḥa* as a whole," it says, "and see what type of mind it reflects or tries to build."[2]

## "Al-Fātiḥa": The Opening

In the Name of God, Most Gracious, Most Merciful.

Praise be to God,
The Cherisher and Sustainer of the Worlds;

Most Gracious, Most Merciful;
Master of the Day of Judgment.

Thee do we worship,
And Thine aid we seek.

Show us the straight way,
The way of those on whom
Thou hast bestowed Thy Grace,
Those whose (portion)
Is not wrath,
And who go not astray.

*The Holy Qur'ān, Sūra 1*

## Signposts on the Road: The Pillars of Islam

For the traveller who sets out on the road of faith, there are certain signposts or pillars by which to chart his way. The Muslim is taught to mark five such pillars.

The first is his witness to the God he serves: the One God, to whom man must submit or surrender totally. The word *Islām* means such surrender, and *Muslim* (*Muslima*) is the man or woman who thus submits to God. This "witness" (*shahāda*) or creed is:

> "There is no god but God (Allāh)
> And Muḥammad is the Prophet of God."

The second of the pillars is prayer.

The third is *zakāt*: the giving of a certain proportion of income for the relief of poverty.

The fourth is the discipline of fasting – from dawn to sunset during the month of Ramaḍān.

The fifth is the pilgrimage to Mecca – to be performed once in a lifetime by every Muslim able to make the journey.

Of these, the duty which most affects the daily life of the Muslim family is the observance of the five daily times of prayer, starting before sunrise and ending late in the evening. In many of the Muslim homes in which I have stayed, the family are up for the Dawn Prayer that begins the day. It should be performed between dawn and sunrise. My hostess in a Cairo club slipped away to a quiet corner after lunch, so that the midday prayer might not be missed. A cheerful schoolgirl, hurrying in to her home with her books under her arm, went first to pray and then to tea. In the cool of the evening in Bombay's beautiful Hanging Gardens, many of the faithful were praying as the sun set.

The midday prayer on Fridays is the weekly congregational gathering. Shops close, business stops. A sermon precedes the prayers, which are performed together without regard to rank. A gallery or aisle in the Mosque is often set apart for women.

There are many who do not pray, and many for whom it is a mere repetition of a formula. The following quotations come from some of those to whom prayer is a reality – individuals in widely differing circumstances.

## The Daily Prayers

In his prayers, a Muslim faces the direction of the city of Mecca. When the time comes, in whatever place he happens to be, he turns towards Mecca and says his prayers. Facing one direction is a symbol of unity of purpose for the millions of Muslims offering their prayers at the same time in the four corners of the earth.

The Muslim says the *Fātiḥa*, and recites any other portion of the Qur'ān he feels like reciting, because of its particular meaning, or because he happens to remember it. Bowing, and touching the earth with his forehead, he terminates with a formal prayer in which he asks God to bless him and his people "as Thou hast blessed Abraham and his people."

The daily prayers are made by practising Muslims individually. A family can join in prayer, or any group which happens to be together. On Fridays, however, the noon prayer should be made collectively.

Dr. Mohammed El-Zayyat, Egyptian diplomat[3]


## The Voice Within

Prayer reminds man of God and helps him to be receptive to His guidance.

The five daily prayers are the best rest intervals for man in our busy and materialistic world.

The moral foundations of Islam are standards in which human behaviour can be channelled for the good of the individual as well as for the good of the community as a whole. They are not mere preaching stuff which may not keep step with ever-changing conditions. They form together that which we call "conscience" or the good side of us.

The "voice within" reminds us always that God is with us. To believe in God is simply the way to develop this "voice within" by seeking God's remembrance, presence and guidance.

Abdel Moghny Said,
Ministry of Manpower, Egypt.[4]

## Man Can Choose

The trouble we now see in the world – and in the Muslim world – is the result of listening to self-will when we should listen to God.

If we ask, what does God say in such a crisis as we face today, we can turn to the Holy Qur'ān and find a key in the verse, "God does not change the condition of a people until the people change themselves." Another key is in the *Fātiḥa*, the prayer we repeat so many times a day. It says, "Guide us in the straight path." This shows us that God wants us to take guidance from Him. If this is so, we have to listen for that guidance. He will not catch us by the ear and drag us along that straight path. We must open our ears to His guidance, which the *Fātiḥa* makes us ask for.

Man is *ashraf al-makhlūqāt*, the top of creation, the highest of living beings. We have freedom to think for ourselves, about what is right and what is wrong. If we say everything is under God's control, we imply that He wills evil. You may say a leaf falls to the ground – and God wills it. But with man's actions it is different. He can choose between right and wrong, which lead to heaven and hell. Therefore we need to ask God's guidance along the straight path.

A time of quiet listening and asking for God's guidance in this way is very important for every Muslim.

Haroun S. Kably,
Advocate, Supreme Court, Delhi, and
President, All India Cutchi Memon Community[5]

Plaited Kufic ornamentation
"God gathers mankind for the Day of Judgment"

# "Thy Lord Hath Not Forsaken Thee . . ."

Verses may be chosen from the Qur'ān as optional acts of prayer to suit the circumstances of the believer, his joy and sorrow, gratitude and need.

A television programme in Cairo on the Prophet's Birthday (April 1973) included a talk on courage in adversity by the newly-appointed Shaikh al-Azhar, Dr Abdul Halim Mahmud. The chapter of the Qur'ān named *The Glorious Morning Light* (Sūra 93) was read. Afterwards a Palestinian lady, a refugee living in Egypt, said:

> As I knit, I pray – just as Gandhi used to say the name of God as he spun. It is the same with the beads you see in my husband's hand. Men say short prayers as they handle them. One of these is, "Your covering and mercy, oh Lord." It means that the inner life is protected. Whatever the circumstances and defeats outside, the life inside our hearts need not be invaded by evil.
>
> One part of the Qur'ān which is often used in our prayers when we are disappointed or disheartened is the sūra called *Al-Doḥā, The Glorious Morning Light*. It is said that these verses were revealed to the Prophet in Mecca, after he had received no revelations for some time and his opponents were mocking him.

By the morning hours
And by the night when it is stillest,
Thy Lord hath not forsaken thee nor doth He hate thee,
And verily the Hereafter will be better for thee than the present,
And verily thy Lord will give unto thee so that thou wilt be content.
Did He not find thee an orphan and protect (thee)?
Did He not find thee wandering and direct (thee)?
Did He not find thee destitute and enrich (thee)?

Therefore the orphan oppress not,
Therefore the beggar drive not away,
Therefore of the bounty of thy Lord be thy discourse.

Mrs Fareeza Taji, Palestine and Cairo[6]

## Prayers for Forgiveness and Obedience

The following come from a prayer-book in use in the Sudan.

O God, I ask forgiveness for myself and for my father; for all Muslims, both men and women; for all believers, both men and women; for those of them who are alive and those of them who are dead.

Deal with me and with them, whether soon or late, in the faith, in this world and the next, according to what You deserve. Do not deal with us, O Lord, according to what we deserve. For You are forgiving, patient, generous, bountiful, tender and merciful.

O God, in Whose hand are all our affairs, put an end to our neglect of You.

We have turned away from You, and from Your Commands, and from listening to the good things You say.

The crime that has caused this is that we have turned towards people who are no concern of ours. These have drawn us away from the benefit of Your speaking with us, and from our fear of You, in spite of our great need of you.

In this there is nothing but loss.

We pray you to turn our desires towards You. For You alone can rescue us from danger in this world and the next.

From *Al-Rātib*, a book of prayers
used by the Imam Muhammad al Mahdi[7]

## The Call to Prayer

God is great! God is great!
I testify that there is no god but God!
I testify that Muḥammad is God's Prophet!
Come to pray! Come to prosperity!
God is great! There is no god but God!

## In the Mosque

Here the believer is a fish in water:
the hypocrite is a caged bird.

Inscription on the gate of the Masjid Jāmi' mosque, Isfahan

# The Fast of Ramaḍān

The Muslim calendar consists of twelve lunar months. Because of this the annual festivals occur at different seasons – thirteen days earlier in each successive year.

The ninth month is the month of fasting, Ramaḍān. All through it, from the first glimpse of the crescent moon to its reappearance a month later to mark the feast, no food or water may be taken from dawn till sunset. Before light, the sound of a drum is often heard in the street, with its summons to awake and eat in the twilight, before a white thread can be distinguished from a black, and the day's fast begins. Ramaḍān is a time of discipline – and also of surprising gaiety, of family visits and neighbourly calls for the *ifṭār* (break-fast) parties in the evenings when the fast is over.

There are various aspects of Ramaḍān. One is the recollection of the revelation of the Qur'ān, especially on the "Night of Power" or "Night of Destiny", the 26th-27th of the month. The Prophet's victories – the Battle of Badr and the conquest of Mecca – are celebrated. It is also a time for the healing of quarrels. This is especially associated with the feast at the end of Ramaḍān. It is customary to greet one's friends by saying, "If I have done you any wrong, please forgive me."

A lady in Djakarta put this into practice. She reached the conclusion that the resentment she held against a friend was in itself wrong – however deeply she felt that she had been injured. She decided to take the opportunity of the feast to set it right on her side. She went to mutual friends and said, "You know how it is between us. Help me." Together they went to the house, and her companions supported her while she apologised for the ill will she had harboured.

The Turkish editor Ahmet Emin Yalman relates a similar incident.

God forgives, and so must we. That is the purpose of the Bairams (feasts). Their function is to be an occasion of reconciliation. This is effective. For instance, when I was engaged, there was a division in my fiancée's family. I noticed that a certain relative was never seen in their company, though I did not know the cause. When the next feast came, the family went to call on the man, there was a sweet reconciliation and all was well.

"I must clean my heart," is a phrase often heard in connection with this kind of action.

The instruction in the Qur'ān about Ramaḍān is as follows. It is reproduced from the leaflet sent out for Ramaḍān 1974 by the Islamic Cultural Centre, London, giving the times of sunrise and sunset in different cities in the United Kingdom, for the benefit of those keeping the Fast.

Ramaḍān is the (month) in which was sent down the Qur'ān, as a Guide to mankind. Also clear (signs), for guidance and for judgment (between right and wrong). So every one of you who is present (at his home) during that month should spend it fasting. But if anyone is ill, or on a journey, the prescribed period (should be made up) by days later. God intends every facility for you. He does not want to put you to difficulties. (He wants you) to complete the prescribed period and to glorify Him.[8]

The feast that follows Ramaḍān lasts three days. It is known as the 'Īd al-fiṭr (Feast of the Breaking of the Fast).


## Payment Due

It is at the end of Ramaḍān that the yearly payment of alms or poor-tax (zakāt) is made. This is defined as "an obligation prescribed by God on those Muslims, men and women, who possess enough means, to distribute a certain percentage of their annual savings or capital in goods or money among the poor and needy."[9]

The basic traditional percentage is 2½ per cent. In recent years zakāt has played a large part in plans for an Islamic economic order and a tax system in line with Islamic tradition.

# CHAPTER TWO

## *The Guide: The Holy Qur'ān*

It is no new tale of fiction, but a confirmation of previous scriptures, and
an explanation of all things, and a
guidance and mercy to those who
believe.

Qur'ān: Sūra 12: 111 *Joseph*

Three voices God Loves:
  The voice of the cock
  The voice of one reading the Qur'ān
  The voice of one seeking pardon
              in the early morning.

Tradition of the Prophet Muḥammad
Quoted by Al-Ghazāli[1]

The guide on the road of life is the Holy Qur'ān.

The revelations that came to the Prophet Muḥammad were written down by his Companions, put in order under his instructions, and finally compiled by the third Caliph 'Uthmān, less than ten years after the Prophet's death. The text is exactly the same now as it was then.

In one book it ranges the whole of life: the worship of God, the nature of man, and the way he should live. It gives both a portrait of creation and instructions by which the individual, the family and the community should conduct their affairs.

The western reader, faced with an English "interpretation", finds himself at a disadvantage. The transition from the original has stripped away its beauty. The unsurpassed music of its language is gone – and the Qur'ān is meant to be *heard*. The vivid word pictures it paints raise no such response as they do in the mind of an Arab reader. Moreover, while it is divided into chapter (*sūra*) and verse, it does not provide a sequence easy to read or to tabulate. It calls for an effort of imagination and study which is difficult to make. The orthodox view that the Qur'ān cannot be translated becomes quickly understandable to anyone who tries to enter into the truth and the experience it conveys.

Nevertheless, from early times the effort at interpretation has been essential for Muslims whose language is other than Arabic. It is the duty of every Muslim to read, and to the best of his ability to understand, the Holy Book. For example, a manuscript centuries old, in the library of Aligarh Muslim University, shows a Persian commentary painstakingly written under the Arabic text in Mogul times. In Istanbul, the "Book Market" has numbers of editions on sale – some of them having the original Arabic transliterated into the modern Turkish script, with a version in Turkish alongside. Translations are appearing in languages ranging from Swahili to Russian and Chinese, including the European languages, with the aim of bringing the Qur'ān to believer and unbeliever alike.

The Prophet's mission: "A mercy for all mankind"

# The Language of the Qur'ān

The language of the Qur'ān, with its dignity, its rhythm, its range and the depth of its meaning, is to the Muslim a part of the miracle of its revelation.

In the remote deserts and tribal communities of Arabia, a rich linguistic vehicle developed, ready to carry a prophetic message to millions and to become the means of expression of a great civilisation.

The Arabic language is built on simple three-letter "roots" which each convey a basic idea and which are developed into an intricate pattern of words covering many shades of meaning. There are only about a thousand of these roots. Human personality enters into each original concept: acting, demanding, co-operating, suffering, seeking and being sought, intense or relaxed. The result is a structure that gives infinite flexibility.

Many of these roots are common to all the Semitic languages. Before Muḥammad's day they had already served mankind well, as the linguistic basis of the early Mesopotamian civilisation, and as the means of expressing the grandeur of Old Testament prophecy. In Arabia the development of language was far richer and more complex. Pre-Islamic poetry used words that convey heroism, joy and sorrow, deep feelings and high ideals – words that were there prepared and ready to carry the inspiration of the Prophet of Arabia to the world.

The dynamic of Arabic is still active. The same original roots are being used to serve the needs of modern science and technology. And while colloquial speech diverges, the classical Arabic – simplified, but in essence the language of the Qur'ān – is heard and understood all over the Arab World. It is the vehicle of radio, television and cinema, and is read in newspapers that may be bought on the streets of any world capital.

What the Qur'ān means to a practising Muslim is explained here by two scholars, one a political scientist and the other a sociologist.

## "The Muslim Lives by the Qur'ān"

"The Muslim lives by the Qur'ān," says Professor Yusuf K. Ibish, Professor of Islamic Political Theory and Institutions in the American University of Beirut. He comes from Damascus, has a Harvard Ph.D., and is a trusted authority on Sufism.

I have not yet come across a western man who understands what the Qur'ān is. It is not a book in the ordinary sense, nor is it comparable to the Bible, either the Old or New Testaments. It is an expression of Divine Will. If you want to compare it with anything in Christianity, you must compare it with Christ Himself. Christ was the expression of the Divine among men, the revelation of the Divine Will. That is what the Qur'ān is. If you want a comparison for the role of Muḥammad, the better one in that particular respect would be Mary. Muḥammad was the vehicle of the Divine, as she was the vehicle. His illiteracy was comparable with her virginity, symbolic of purity. There are western orientalists who have devoted their life to the study of the Qur'ān, its text, the analysis of its words, discovering that this word is Abyssinian, that word is Greek by origin. The Bible and other literary works have also been subjected to this treatment. But all this is immaterial. The Qur'ān was divinely inspired, then it was compiled, and what we have now is the expression of God's Will among men. That is the important point.

One has to make an effort to understand. Like the bride behind the veil the Holy Qur'ān does not lend itself easily to the seeker. You can read it as you would read any book, and you will gather certain things from it. But to grasp its message truly, you have to penetrate from the external appearance to the inner reality, from the exoteric to the esoteric meaning. It is a two-level process, and of course one needs the guidance of those who know.

The Muslim lives by the Qur'ān. From the first rituals of birth to the principal events of life and death, marriage, inheritance, business contracts: all are based on the Qur'ān. A man can live and die decently if he seeks inspiration from the Qur'ān. Most people from outside look on it as a small book containing limited instruction about conduct and life. This is not so. There are guiding principles, and you can unfold any number of valid interpretations.

Professor Yusuf Ibish, Beirut[2]

# A Motivator of Thought

Dr Ali Issa Othman is one of a Palestinian family coming from a village near Jerusalem, one of those divided by the armistice-line of 1948. He was educated in Chicago, where he took a Doctorate in Sociology. He was for some years Adviser to UNRWA[3] on Education, and in particular on social studies. His book, *The Concept of Man in Islam, in the writings of Al-Ghazāli*, was published in Cairo in 1960. He says:

> The Qur'ān is organic in ideas – not in structure. Get away from the idea of a book that starts and develops. When you have read it all, then you have everything. You can pick it up and start reading it anywhere.
>
> It appeals to common people as well as scholars. My mother is illiterate and she has an enjoyment of the Qur'ān that I perhaps do not have: the music of it. My understanding can get in the way. She and my father always used to pray. They were disturbed if they could not get their ablutions done in time to pray the evening prayer before the sun set, or if ever they slept after the sun had risen. As a child, I used to open my eyes every morning in our Palestine village and see them at prayer. The younger generation who have been to school know and understand the words, but miss the feeling my parents had.
>
> We cannot see Muslim thought in the right perspective unless we appreciate and understand the Qur'ān as a motivator of thought and an end of knowledge. Without such understanding, the student of Muslim thought must continue to work in the dark. It is in the direct impact of the Qur'ān on the Muslim mind that we may discover those unwritten, but perhaps most important and fundamental, orientations towards truth and human ends. In these orientations lie the Muslims' general sense of history and change, their peculiar sense of time, and their peculiar sense of purpose in seeking knowledge.
>
> Truth in itself and outside man's knowledge does not have a biography of development. Only the individual's understanding of it has. Thus there is permanence in truth and change in understanding. The history of Muslim thought in general cannot be fully understood by an "evolutionary" approach to the history of ideas. The truth which is essential for happiness is supposed by Muslims to be all there and complete – in the Qur'ān and the *Sunna*, (the tradition and practice of the Prophet).

Dr Ali Issa Othman, Palestine and Beirut[4]

# Towards Understanding the Qur'ān

One of the most influential Twentieth Century commentaries on the Qur'ān is that by Sayyid Abul A'lā Mawdūdī (1903–1979). Written in Urdu, this massive work of scholarship was produced in the midst of the struggles for independence and the early years of Pakistan. It is entitled *Tafhīm al-Qur'ān* (Towards Understanding the Qur'ān). He undertook the task in 1941 and completed it in 1973, six volumes and thirty years later, strenuous years of leadership and controversy. A full English translation is appearing.[5]

The following extracts from Mawdūdī's Preface are taken from *Translations From The Quran*, made on the basis of Mawdūdī's work by Altaf Gauhar, author and Editor-in-Chief of *South* magazine and *Third World Quarterly*, published from London. "These translations were undertaken at a time when the only book to which I had access was the Qur'ān," he says.

> *Tafhīm al-Qur'ān* is not a literal translation of the original text. It is an attempt to present the meanings of the Qur'ān in plain language keeping the historical perspective in view. The Qur'ān speaks to you in the language of life, vividly and melodiously: by comparison the language of translation is a poor echo of the glorious original ... one is left cold and begins to wonder whether this is indeed the Book which has no equal.
>
> The Qur'ān is great literature as it is great instruction. Its words go straight to the heart and it is this quality which, like a crack of lightning, shook the length and breadth of Arabia.
>
> The Qur'ān presents an arrangement which is completely contrary to our expectations. We find beliefs, precepts, orders, criticisms, warnings, promises, arguments, evidence, historical illustrations and references to natural phenomena following one another in rapid succession without any apparent regard for logic ... It talks of the origin of man, the structure of the earth and the heavens ... It recalls the beliefs and criticizes the conduct of different nations, analyses metaphysical problems and refers to many other things. The object however is not to give lessons in metaphysics, philosophy, history or any other science, but to remove misunderstandings about reality ... to acquaint (man) with the result of actions which conflict with its underlying principles.
>
> Whether one is a believer or not, as a rational person one must read this book by taking into account the fundamental assumptions made in the book itself, and by the Prophet who presented it to the world.[6]

# The Qur'ān and the Prophets

No less than eight chapter headings in the Qur'ān recall figures in the Old and New Testaments. Moses and Jesus, founders of Judaism and Christianity, are prophets like Muḥammad with the title of *rasūl* (apostle), greater than *nabī* (announcer).

In the course of the Qur'ān, David and Solomon receive no less than thirty-three mentions, and Noah appears some thirty times, as well as heading a chapter. The Sūra of Joseph is the longest narrative given. Jonah, "the Man of the Fish", and Sheba, whose famous Queen visits Solomon, are both names of Sūras.

Many of the stories are allusive rather than narratory. Evidently the facts were well known to the hearers, and the commentators fill in the details. Some of the information given is found in Jewish sources other than the Old Testament, and in the case of Jesus in the Apocryphal Gospels. The lives of the prophets were current knowledge in Muḥammad's day, as they have continued to be throughout the Muslim world.

In one chapter of the Qur'ān (Sūra 6: 83–86 *Cattle*) eighteen prophets are named. The authoritative modern commentary by Abdullah Yusuf Ali analyses these in four groups.[7] They cover, he says, the great teachers accepted among the three religions based on Moses, Jesus and Muḥammad. First come Abraham, Isaac and Jacob. Then follow those who "led active lives and are called 'doers of good'." These are Noah, David and Solomon, Job and Joseph, Moses and Aaron. In contrast, the next group were not men of action but preachers of truth who led solitary lives. They include Zachariah and his son John (the Baptist), Jesus and Elias (Elijah), and their designation is "the righteous". Finally come four who were concerned in the clash of nations, and who through conflict and personal misfortune kept to the path of God: Ishmael, Elisha, Jonah and Lot.

The chapter headed *The Prophets* (Sūra 21) has a similar passage. Elsewhere over and over again the historic sequence is repeated – a warning, followed by either repentance or destruction, as God sends His messengers to one nation after another. The view of history in the Muslim mind is a prophetic one.

According to the Qur'ān, the succession of prophets has been completed – sealed – by the mission of Muḥammad. The truth necessary for man to live by has been revealed. There is no need for more. But if men do not presume to claim the stature of the prophets, there is still plenty of scope for humbly following their example. Muhammad's own constant emphasis that he was only a man like other men lays stress on the responsibility carried by all believers.

Here is one of many passages which show the heritage of prophetic inspiration common to Muslim, Jew and Christian.

> We inspire thee [Muḥammad] as We inspired Noah and the prophets after him, as We inspired Abraham and Ishmael and Isaac and Jacob and the tribes, and Jesus and Job and Jonah and Aaron and Solomon, and as We imparted unto David the Psalms;
>
> And messengers We have mentioned unto thee before, and messengers We have not mentioned unto thee; and Allah spake direct unto Moses;
>
> Messengers of good cheer and of warning, in order that mankind might have no argument against Allah after the messengers. Allah was ever Mighty, Wise.
>
> Qur'ān: Sūra 4: 163–165 *Women*

Qur'ān stand, *raḥl*, usually found in mosques
Turkestan, 1360 AD

# CHAPTER THREE

# *The Pilgrim Road*

In the Name of God be the
course and the mooring.

Prayer of Noah as he launched the ark,
and of pilgrims as they set out for Mecca.
Qur'ān: Sūra 11: 41 *Hūd*

I come with many sins
From a far land ...
O God, this Sanctuary is Thy Sacred Place.

Prayer on entering the gates of Mecca[1]

Once at least in a lifetime, every Muslim capable of doing so is supposed to pack his bag, leave his home and take the road for Mecca; Mecca, to which his thoughts have turned every day since in childhood he learned to pray.

Over a million people go there each year, most of them during the month of pilgrimage. In 1980, the total had risen to 1,900,000 and about half of these came from outside Saudi Arabia. The Saudi government keeps a register of pilgrims from other countries. In 1968 these were 318,507; in 1969, 406,895. In 1974, out of a total of 1,484,975, the number from outside Arabia was 918,777.[2]

Much of this human torrent flows through Jedda, with its modern airport and deep-water harbour. More and more come by air: 532,000 in 1979, 572,000 in 1980. This involves handling up to 50,000 arrivals a day during the short and hectic period just before the Ḥajj. To meet this challenge Jedda's immense airport, dedicated in April 1981, includes a special Ḥajj Terminal, imaginatively constructed like a huge tent. Here the pilgrims can enter, wait to meet their guides, and find transport by road on the final stage of their journey to Mecca.

Every contrast of colour and costume, class and race is to be seen, but to enter Mecca all are dressed alike in two sheets of unsewn white cloth. External trappings and all things superficial are laid aside. King and peasant, descendant of the Prophet and newest African convert, all are equal in this demonstration of brotherhood – and sisterhood. Women, never veiled on pilgrimage, take full part.

The King moves from Riyadh to lead the pilgrimage and entertain rulers and ambassadors of Muslim states. Informal discussions on policy and action are an important element. The Saudi Arabian government moves its headquarters to Mecca, and a considerable part of the oil wealth of the country has gone into modernising the arrangements for the reception of so vast a crowd.

Health precautions have turned what used to be a hazardous journey into a still rigorous but comparatively safe undertaking. Strict quarantine regulations, hospitals and mobile clinics, water supplies, drinking taps by roads along which almost a million must walk in a day: all these help the health record, and there have been no serious epidemics in recent years.

In the 1970's, a programme of building completed the expansion of the Great Mosque itself, so that 300,000 pilgrims can gather in its court at one time, each with a clear view of the square-built, black-draped building at its centre, the Ka'ba. Tradition dates the worship of God here back to the days of Abraham.[3]

No non-Muslim may enter Mecca. Soon after the day when the Prophet re-entered the city and cleansed the sanctuary of its idols — and before his own Pilgrimage of Farewell — it was closed to any but followers of Islam.


## Father Abraham

The pilgrimage rites recall two events: the story of Abraham and the Farewell Pilgrimage made by the Prophet shortly before his death.

The Patriarch and Prophet Abraham travelled the desert caravan routes linking the centres of early civilisation: the same routes along which, through the past fourteen centuries, millions of pilgrims have passed — destination Mecca. More important, he travelled the road from the worship of many gods to that of the One Creator. The stories of his family, of his break with idols and his finding faith in *the* God, Allāh, are told in the Qur'ān.

Muḥammad regarded himself as the restorer of the pure faith in One God first pioneered by Abraham, the spiritual father of the three great monotheistic faiths, as well as the ancestor of the Jews and of many Arabs; cousins whose destiny has been closely linked in history ever since.

According to Meccan tradition, the sanctuary there was first built by Abraham and his son Ismāʿīl (Ishmael). To reach Mecca from Damascus took later pilgrim caravans forty days. Hebron, where Abraham settled and where his tomb is venerated by Muslim, Jew and Christian alike, is nearer still. The journey to Mecca would not be a long one for such a traveller.

There, it is said, he took Hagar when she was turned out by Sarah. Her frenzied search for water was rewarded by the bubbling up of a spring, Zamzam, from which every pilgrim drinks. Her desperate wanderings are recalled in the running to and fro of pilgrims between the two hillsides of Marwa and Ṣafā. The climax of the Pilgrimage is the Feast of Sacrifice (ʿĪd al-Aḍḥā). This is in honour of Abraham's willingness to sacrifice his son. If they can afford it, Muslim families all over the world kill a sheep or other animal at this time, and give part of the meat to the poor.

# The Significance of Ḥajj

The Arabic word *ḥajj* means "to set out for a definite purpose". Specifically, it refers to the pilgrimage to the city of Mecca. A *Ḥājji* is one who has performed the Pilgrimage. An Islamic Correspondence Course, edited by Ḥājji Riadh El-Droubie and issued by Minaret House, London, devotes one unit to the Ḥajj. The story of Abraham and his readiness to sacrifice his son is quoted from the Qur'ān. Many, but not all, Muslim commentators think that the son in the story is Ishmael, but the text might refer either to him or to Isaac.

The spirit of Ḥajj is the spirit of total sacrifice: sacrifice of personal comforts, worldly pleasures, acquisition of wealth, companionship of relatives and friends, vanities of dress and personal appearance, pride relating to birth, national origin, accomplishments, work or social status.

This sacrifice of self was attained to the highest degree by the Prophet Abraham (peace be on him) who is known as "The Friend of God" (*Khalīl Allāh*). The story of his sacrifice is narrated in the Qur'ān in the following manner:

> (Abraham said) "O my Lord! Grant me a righteous (son)." So We gave him the good news of a boy ready to suffer and forbear.
>
> Then, when the son reached (the age of serious) work with him, he said, "O my son! I see in vision that I offer you in sacrifice: now see what is your view."
>
> The son said: "O my father! Do as you are commanded. You will find me, if God so wills, one practising patience and constancy."
>
> So when they had both submitted their wills (to God), and he (Abraham) had laid him (Ishmael) prostrate on his forehead (for sacrifice), We called out to him: "O Abraham! You have already fulfilled the vision."
>
> Thus indeed do We reward those who do right. For this was obviously a trial. And We ransomed him with a great sacrifice. And We left (this blessing) for him among generations (to come) in later times: "Peace and salutation to Abraham!"
>
> Qur'ān: Sūra 37: 100–109 *The Ranks*

Although the events to which this narrative refers occurred many centuries ago . . . the spirit of submission to God cannot be illustrated for us in any clearer manner.

"Ḥajj" also signifies the brotherhood of all Muslims, demonstrated in this greatest of all international assemblies . . . (It) reminds Muslims of the forthcoming assembly on the Day of Judgment . . . and also of the birth, rise and expansion of Islam, the overthrow of idolatry, the establishment of the worship of one God, and the difficulties and accomplishments of the Prophet Muḥammad (peace be on him) and the early Muslims.[4]

Dish: "The ships that run upon the sea at God's command"
Turkey, c. 1630 AD

# Motives for the Pilgrimage

Since 1960 the number of pilgrims from outside Arabia has more than trebled. Modern means of transport facilitate but cannot fully explain this increase.

What draws the pilgrims? Here are answers from a number of Muslims.

The leader of twenty thousand Iranian pilgrims: Abulfazl Hazeghi, educator and parliamentarian:

> The purpose of the Pilgrimage is to clean the heart. A pilgrim has to set right anything wrong between him and another person, to make his will and to pay his debts. When he leaves home he should be free of debt, hate, bitterness, resentment, impurity.
>
> Personally, I had three times the honour to take about twenty thousand pilgrims from Iran to Mecca. I have seen many people getting a new direction of life – completely different; some of them paying a large part of their wealth to be used for people's welfare, for the building of mosques, hospitals, clinics, etc. I was witness to many restorations between man and man, sect and sect, removing all kinds of misunderstanding and creating new friendships.

A professor:

> I have been several times to Mecca. I went with one idea, and came back with another. I looked forward to seeing the places where the Prophet lived and worked. I found more than that: the vast concourse of people from many lands, all the same, all equal; and their yearning for God, as all move round the Ka'ba, hundreds of thousands of us together.

A former prime minister:

> I have been three times – twice for the Ḥajj. The simplicity of it is inspiring. But Muslims miss something of what it could be. It could be a conference at which everything of importance to Muslims is dealt with. The Prophet used it in this way. At his last pilgrimage, he made a great speech which is a charter for all Muslims.

An Egyptian lady:

> It is like a rehearsal for Resurrection Day – everybody equal, all kinds of people together, the whole of humanity before God.

An article addressed to London students faces the difficulties encountered by pilgrims. Mecca has its dust and flies, its colds and coughs, its taxi-drivers and watersellers who are cynics. "Ḥajj does need preparation and training," says the writer. He urges an imaginative use of television and radio to introduce different groups of Muslims to each other – in place of the sometimes incongruous mingling of sermons and western dance music. He concludes:

> Ḥajj has maintained the capacity to lift man from the jumble of his preoccupations and out of the mechanical framework within which he lives. Never is prayer offered with a greater feeling. In the unending flow of worshippers around the Ka'ba throughout the day and throughout the night, there is satisfaction to the heart, joy to the eye, and mystery to the soul . . .
>
> The scorched and barren landscape synchronises perfectly with these feelings of the pilgrim and even helps to produce them. It could never have done so were it cool and green and luscious. Yet there is no debasement, but ardour and grandeur.
>
> The days of the Ḥajj are indeed unique days. Would that its great possibilities are realised![5]

## Mecca Airlift

During the pilgrimage season hundreds of planes are chartered to bring pilgrims from every continent. Typical is one that started from Britain, in February 1968.

In the bitter cold of London's wintry dockland, the party gathers at the East London Mosque. It is an illustration both of the breadth of the Muslim world, and of the variety of Britain's multi-racial society. Pakistanis and Indians are in the majority. A number of Iranians move together. Somaliland, Zanzibar, Kenya and Nigeria are represented among the Africans.

Gayest note on a grey day is the emerald head-scarf of a Nigerian woman. She is one of a party of Nigerian students. Her husband says:

> Three months ago nothing was farther from my mind than the Ḥajj. I had lost all faith and grip on life. But my brother's son never stopped coming to see me, and in the end he helped me to make a fresh start. I am going home in a few months. I began to think, "I cannot take home the bad ways I have learned here," and I decided to clean up my life. Now my mother is coming from Lagos, and we shall meet in Mecca and make the pilgrimage together.

Among the party is an exiled ruler. An old man from Guyana is seen off by his son and daughter-in-law, immigrants to Britain. He has stayed with them for two weeks on his way. It is his first journey and he is nervous, as is an elderly Turk whose womenfolk are comforting him. The wife of the caretaker of the mosque encourages the lonely, and sees that everyone has the necessary documents. She is Welsh. She became a Muslim twenty-seven years ago and has, she says, prayed the regular five times a day ever since. Her warm heart, common sense, box of medicines and knowledge of Mecca will stand the others in good stead. Youngest of the party is a fifteen-year-old schoolgirl, travelling with her mother and her father, who has a business in Lancashire.

The women wait in a room above the mosque. Five coaches are at the door. Before they leave, the Call to Prayer is sounded, sheets are rapidly laid on the floor, and all pray. One woman starts to sing – reciting the verses of the Qur'ān which her Urdu pilgrimage book recommends.

Bags and people are piled into the coaches, and they are away. Tomorrow morning they will be in Jedda, the next day in Mecca.


## The Discipline of Ḥajj

In a talk to would-be pilgrims in London, it was said, "There is no beauty in the Holy Land. You go to please God, not yourself." While the hardship is now lessened, the Pilgrimage remains a severe physical ordeal. The lunar months of the Muslim calendar come round at different seasons of the year, and the Ḥajj often takes place in intense summer heat. Any loss of temper or any altercation destroys its value.

There are many books designed to help pilgrims find their way through the month they spend in Arabia. A recent one comes from Dr Hassan Hathout, Egyptian doctor. It is a commonsense document, combining advice on health and diet with spiritual background. Dr Hathout stresses the permanent gain in tolerance and self-restraint.

The journey of Ḥajj is not easy. It is a taxing process and I do not speak in terms of the distance you cover from Home to Ḥajj. Coming together with a few hundred thousand people within a limited span of time and space, having to perform the same rites, entailing mass movements in a limited time from one place to another, is an ordeal. Yet the main cause of difficulty is the human one. These people have many different backgrounds and customs, do not speak the same language, and yet they are gathered into this colossal human mass. One can imagine that endless situations would arise all loaded with nervous tension and intolerance. Yet strong "brakes" are placed on any tendency to nervousness or intolerance – it is a criterion of pilgrimage to be pure and tolerant. The Qur'ān says: "The Ḥajj season comprises the specified months. He who proposes to do Ḥajj in them must abstain from obscenity, wickedness and ill-tempered disputes during Ḥajj."

However provoked, you should remain gentle and tolerant. This attitude of peace and forgiveness is imposed by your own self – and you do not pretend to be tolerant, but you feel you really are. This is indeed a great exercise in self-restraint and self-exploration – for you will sometimes be surprised to discover your tremendous faculties for love and patience, thus unearthing treasures you can count on in your future life.

Some of us who are highly sophisticated, especially those with western upbringing, do time and again . . . voice many complaints . . . (but) it seems to me that one of the aims of Ḥajj is to put the one Nation together in the one pot and make them mix and mingle . . . The privileged cast away their arrogance and pride because they know it is a sin to be harsh to your brother or be scornful of him . . . It is democracy in practice – and it is democracy in love – under God . . . It is true that some Muslims live in circumstances precluding them from attaining the standard that would please. Instead of being angry with them we should be angry for them.

Dr Hassan Hathout, Egypt and Kuwait[6]

# The Prophet's Farewell Pilgrimage

One of the great events of Islamic history took place during Muḥammad's last pilgrimage, shortly before his death. He addressed his followers in a speech that was the climax of his mission. This speech, made in dialogue with his hearers, has come down as a summary of his message. Every biographer of the Prophet describes the event, and every pilgrim recalls it as he follows the course of the Ḥajj in the Prophet's footsteps.

The crowd, an estimated one hundred thousand, gathered at Arafat, a few miles outside Mecca, as it does today. Muḥammad rode the same favourite camel, Al Kaswa, that had carried him as a fugitive from Mecca to Medina ten years earlier. By his side was Bilal, the negro ex-slave whose great voice had won the honour of giving the first call to prayer on behalf of the Prophet. His voice, picked up by others through the crowd, was the relay-system by which the words of Muḥammad reached the whole assembly.[7]

Then came the last verse of the Qur'ān to be revealed:

This day have I perfected your religion for you, completed My favour upon you, and have chosen for you Islam as your religion.

*Qur'ān: Sūra 5: 4 The Table*

In the course of this address, the Prophet called for the wiping out of vendettas – starting with a blood-feud in his own family as an example. This may be compared with Moses' farewell speech to the men and women of the Exodus, when he said, "Vengeance is mine, saith the Lord, I will repay." (*Deuteronomy* 32:35)

Among many summaries of this speech, here is one designed for teaching children and students. It comes from *An Easy History of the Prophet of Islam*, published in Lahore.

1. All the customs and practices of the pagan age are abolished.

2. All compensation for bloodshed of the old days is abolished: and on behalf of my family I declare illegal the indemnity for the blood of Ibn Rabī'a ibn Hārith [murdered cousin of the Prophet].

3. All usuries of the past are wiped out.

4. Fear God in respect of women. You, men, have your rights over your wives and they have their rights over you.

5. As regards your slaves, be fair to them. Give them to eat what you eat and to wear what you wear.

6. Your blood and your properties are as sacred for one another as are this day, this month and this place.

7. Each Muslim is a brother of another. All Muslims form one brotherhood.

8. An Arab has no superiority over a non-Arab, nor has a non-Arab over an Arab. You are all born of Adam, and Adam was made out of clay.

9. Whoever is entrusted with a thing belonging to another must deliver his trust to its owner.

10. The debtors must pay their debts.

11. I leave behind one thing, and you will never go astray if you hold it fast, and that is the Book of God.[8]

Pilgrims at Mecca encircle the *Ka'ba*

## Three Holy Cities: Mecca, Medina and Al-Quds (Jerusalem)

Mecca, Medina and Jerusalem are all holy places to the Muslim. Almost every pilgrim to Mecca also visits Medina (225 miles northwest of Mecca), where the Prophet Muḥammad lived for ten years and was buried.

Through the centuries, pilgrims to Mecca have regarded a visit to Jerusalem as a completion of their pilgrimage. The city is known in Arabic as Bait al-Maqdis (the Holy House), or Al-Quds.

There Muslim and Christian pilgrims have sought the same holy places. When the end of the Ḥajj has coincided with Easter, large numbers of pilgrims of both faiths have often mingled in the streets. The writer was among them in 1966, the year before the Six Day War.

The Christian shrines were visited by the Muslim pilgrims. One party from Iraq were heard in disappointed argument because a service prevented them from entering the cave in the Church of the Nativity in Bethlehem where by tradition Jesus was born. They had just been to Hebron, to the ancient mosque which marks the tomb of Abraham. From some countries, there were pilgrim parties of both faiths: from Nigeria, for instance, and Yugoslavia. The parked coaches from the latter country might carry either Christians or Muslims.

The streets of the Old City were brightly lit, the shops open all night. Many homes had been opened to house the thousands from Syria and Egypt who, with the Cypriots, formed the mass of Christian pilgrims. Alongside these Christian homes were those with gay pictures chalked on the doors to welcome home Ḥājjis. *Ḥajj mabrūr wa dhanab maghfūr.* "Pilgrimage made and sins forgiven." Less edifying were the second-hand clothes markets outside Herod's Gate and at the coach park, where Europe's old coats were finding their way to remote villages and Bedouin camps.

For the Muslims, all these things were incidental to the visit to Al-Masjid al-Aqsā, the Farthest Mosque, revered by the Prophet; the place towards which his prayers were first directed, and the starting point of his great mystical experience, the journey into heaven, during which he received the revelation about the five daily times of prayer. This event is known as the "Night of Ascent", and is said to have inspired Dante.

About one fifth of the area of the Old City is taken up with the courts of the Noble Sanctuary, Al-Ḥaram al-Sharīf, with its large congregational Mosque, Al-Aqsā, to the south, and in the centre the marvel of the Dome of the Rock. In 1966, repairs and restoration had just been completed. The fresh gold on the dome dominated the landscape and the city. A tall crane still stood by its side, and the little Dome of the Chain awaited repair, its condition a measure of the extent of the work done on the larger structure.

Every Muslim child knows the story of the Arab capture of Jerusalem. In AD 638 the Patriarch in the beleaguered city offered to surrender it, but only to the Caliph 'Umar in person. 'Umar, simply dressed, entered the city and said his prayers not in, but near, the Church of the Holy Sepulchre, so that his followers might not be tempted to take it over. The treaty he made is regarded as a model of tolerance. This and the parallel story of the reconquest of the city by Saladin (Salāḥ ad-dīn) after a century of Christian occupation are viewed in sharp contrast with the bloodshed and slaughter associated with the Frankish armies in 1099 when the Crusaders took the city.

The Dome of the Rock, first of the great architectural achievements of Islam, was finished by the ninth caliph, Abdel Malik, in the year AD 691. In its thirteen centuries of life, it has been fortunate in its restorations. Each, including the most recent, has kept to the character of the building and has enhanced its beauty. As with other great works of art, it has a perfection which is, in its own sphere, unsurpassed.

The care of Al-Aqsā and the Noble Sanctuary is the trust of a group of families whose tenure goes back eight hundred years, though many were exiled after 1967. They were installed by Saladin after he recaptured Jerusalem from the Crusaders in AD 1189. Khatibs, Husseinis and Nashashibis have lived in the houses overlooking the Noble Sanctuary ever since, and generation has followed generation in its service. Some have been there longer still. Khalidis – the family of the great general Khalid ibn Walid – have resided in the city since AD 638. More recent comers are Shihabis, who arrived from Lebanon three centuries ago. To them are entrusted the Prophet's cloak and pen, precious relics which are shown to the faithful each year on the Night of Ascent, Muḥammad's mystical journey to heaven.

In the Dome of the Rock, human skill and artistry surround something unique in its rugged simplicity. The stretch of bare rock beneath the dome is a stark reminder of a Greatness no image can evoke, which commands the total submission of man's every gift and talent.

The rock is linked with Abraham. Centuries after his time, David bought it, and Solomon built his temple here. In these courts Jesus walked and taught. No place on earth has been the focus of so much faith and so much hope. It is central to all three of the great monotheistic faiths. They have a basic kinship stemming from Father Abraham.

Co-operation between Jews, Christians and Muslims was the hope of the Prophet Muḥammad. He was disappointed, but his respect for others who believe and obey God is deeply rooted in the Muslim mind.

Prayer niche, *mihrāb*, showing direction of Mecca
Round the arch are the first verses of the Qur'ān: *Al-Fātiḥa*
Iran, 1226 AD

# PART TWO
*The Community*

# CHAPTER FOUR
## *Principles of Community Life*

The believers are brothers.

Qur'ān: Sūra 49: 10 *The Apartments*

None of you can be a believer unless
he loves for his brother what he loves
for himself.

Tradition of the Prophet Muḥammad

Muḥammad was both a prophet and a ruler. The first few years of his mission were spent in his native Mecca. It was a flourishing centre of trade, and persecution grew as one person after another joined him in a way of life that threatened the prevailing materialism.

To escape assassination, he and his followers moved to Medina. There for ten years he ruled a community which has always been regarded as the embryo of the Islamic state. He was succeeded by four of his close companions, the "just" caliphs: Abu Bakr, 'Umar, 'Uthmān and 'Alī.

The role of the Prophet as a social reformer, and of the first Muslim community in Medina as a social order, are still a stimulus to political thought in the Muslim world.

This section gives one man's answer to the question, "What does the life of the Prophet of Islam mean to us today?": and another man's insight into the relation between an individual and the community to which he belongs.


## What Does the Life of the Prophet Mean to Us?

Each year the Birthday of the Prophet gives an opportunity for general rejoicing and family parties, and also for fresh assessment of the role of Muḥammad and of the relevance of his life and message to contemporary needs.

One such assessment was made in the mosque at Zürich, on the occasion of the Prophet's Birthday, 1972, by Dr Ismail Izzet Hassan, Doctor of Music and formerly of Cairo.

> Fourteen centuries ago, in a land which was at that time backward and out-of-the-way, a successful and happily married young business-man retired to Mount Hirā near Mecca to pursue quiet meditation. At the age of forty he was shaken to his depths by a vision of the Archangel Gabriel, and after that he understood that God had chosen him as a prophet.
>
> When he died at the age of sixty-three, his life's work had completely transformed his native land. Not only did a new, pure faith prevail. The whole of existence had become different. The status of the poor and of the slaves, the rights of women, the protection of minors, had been put on a totally new basis; politics and economy were reorganised, democracy brought into public life, all in a manner incredibly audacious for those days.

A hundred years after the quiet meditation of Mount Hirā, Islam had spread a new civilisation from Central Asia to the Atlantic. It challenged other civilisations to rid themselves of decadence and barbarism. One single man had initiated a revolution and a renaissance that had spread across the known world. How was this possible?

The Prophet of Islam always maintained that he was only a man like all others, but that he had been called by God to be His messenger and God had revealed His Word, the Holy Qur'ān, to him. The secret of Muhammad's effectiveness lies in his complete obedience to his Lord, in his total self-dedication to the execution of the instructions he received from Him. He did not fulfil his task out of his own strength, but as an instrument of a Higher Power. A *Hadīth* (tradition of the Prophet) says: "My Lord has formed my character and formed it well."

No personal ambition drove him on. Again and again it cost him great inner struggles and conquest of self to hold to his mission. Temptations, crushing difficulties, bitter enemies opposed him. Dedicated friends helped him. He experienced successes, some of which could hardly have been expected by human foresight. First he arose to proclaim a faith. Later he acted as law-giver, as head of state, as military commander. He was a husband and a father, as well as a friend and counsellor to many people. He was active in the world – a human, like us – yet always completely for God.

In this manner the Prophet Muhammad fulfilled the true task of Man, the purpose of humanity, and so he is also called "the perfect human" (*al-insānu-'l-kāmil*). According to Islamic teaching, God has appointed Man as His agent on earth, has made him responsible for executing His Will and commanded him to stand up for Good against Evil. The Prophet taught the Muslims in the new community which grew around him how to live and be effective in this manner.

The Founder of Islam has not only shown a way to salvation in a future life, but has also brought practical answers to the problems of this life. He leaves us not only a theory that is preached, but concrete experience and historical facts.

And we do need concrete facts. In today's situation of crisis the call for renewal, change and progress is heard everywhere. The Prophet Muhammad is a prime example of a personality who understood how to bring about revolutionary progress and build a community of true brotherhood.

The deep trouble and distress in today's world may have a simple root cause: that we humans – and, unfortunately, we must also add, we Muslims too – have not properly obeyed God's essential instructions and thereby have missed our main goal. Whoever studies the life of the Holy Prophet of Islam in earnest finds himself confronted with the question: "Are you also ready to follow the highest that God shows you?"

The name *Muḥammad* is repeated in this design

# Individual Versus Society

There are two sources of social legislation in Islam. One is the Qur'ān, which contains the laws on which life in Muhammad's Medina was built. The second is the *Sunna*, the "custom" of the Prophet: what he said and what he did. His personal life was recorded in detail by his family and friends. Each of his sayings is known as a "tradition", *ḥadīth*.

Dr Hassan Hathout, writer, poet and surgeon, illustrates his theme, "Individual versus Society", by examples drawn from the experience of the Prophet and his immediate successors. These stories are part of the furniture of the mind of every Muslim — told to children as well as studied by lawyers. They are, he says, "formative elements in the Muslim mentality."[1]

In our present-day world, both the capitalist and the communist camps suffer from a conflict between the right of the individual and the right of the community. Whereas capitalist societies protect the individual and his rights, often pushing this so far as to trespass on communal welfare, communist countries almost disregard the individuality of the individual for the sake of society as a whole. The results of both are far from satisfactory.

The so-called "free world" boasts of political freedom, and freedom of thought and expression. Yet under the banner of private enterprise such perversions as greed and selfishness have become acceptable. Freedom to become rich has often added to the miseries of the poor. Freedom of thought has often been converted into freedom to pollute thought. As people become more and more material-minded, they become less and less God-guided. The result is an unhappy society.

When we turn to communist societies, the scene is even worse. Individuals are but the bricks used for a building. Society looks like a beehive or an ant colony — very active, very disciplined. In this atmosphere, a sign of individuality is looked upon as political opposition. Since the conception of God is non-existent, it is difficult to imagine any source from which values such as conscience, love, self-restraint and charity can derive. The inevitable result is also an unhappy society.

It seems that both sides have been willing to reconsider their systems. The communist camp has had to permit some kinds of private ownership. In capitalist countries it has been found inevitable to impose certain limitations on the absolute rights of the individual: rising taxation, state ownership, the welfare state, for example.

The ideal ratio of individual to communal interest has not yet been found. Against this background, it may be asked how Islam views this question. It is interesting to note that the views here given are not derived from the theories of communism and capitalism. The religion of Islam as conveyed by the Prophet Muḥammad is nearly fourteen hundred years old.

The communal and individual viewpoints have been so blended in Islam that it is difficult to separate them. Fraternity and love are the cement which binds various individuals to form a society. In the Prophet's words: "The faithful are to one another like (parts of) a building – each part strengthening the others." And: "The faithful in their mutual compassion, sympathy and love are exemplified by the whole body. If one of its organs falls ill, the remainder will suffer."

These ideas are not merely of moral value. They are legally implemented, for Islam brought with it a legal system. A legal principle introduced by the second caliph 'Umar decrees that if a person dies of starvation, the penalty for wrongful death should be imposed on all the citizens of the town, as though they had killed him.

## Duties and Rights

Many of the teachings of Islam bear a dual nature. An individual's right may also be his duty, and as such cannot be surrendered. Islam thus protects vital communal rights by asking the individual to be clear about his own rights.

*The right to be educated* – recognised by law – is also the duty to learn. The Prophet said: "Seeking knowledge is a duty for every Muslim, man or woman."

*The right to express an opinion* involves the duty to speak out. If you believe that something is right, you have not the right to remain silent about it. The Prophet teaches: "He who remains silent about truth is a dumb devil." Related to this is the duty to give testimony in court, and this may also be applied to the duty to vote. The Qur'ān says: "Do not withhold testimony, and whoever does so must have a wrongful heart."[2]

*The right of political opposition* and of honest criticism of authorities is also a duty. The first caliph, Abu Bakr, in his inaugural speech, said: "If I do right, support me. If I do wrong, correct me." The second caliph, 'Umar, asked: "What will you do if I go wrong?" One of those present stood up and shouted: "By God, we will put you right with the edge of our swords." 'Umar replied: "If you do not do so, you will lose God's blessing. And if I do not accept your correction, I shall lose God's blessing."

This attitude is not confined to political issues, but concerns every aspect of life, in accordance with the saying of the Prophet: "Whoever sees wrong being done must change it – with his hand, if he can, or else with his tongue or his heart." Even obedience to government, commendable as it is in Islam, may become a crime if the government disobeys God. The Prophet said: "There is no obedience if it entails disobedience to God." The first caliph declared: "Obey me as long as I obey God. If I disobey Him, then you owe me no obedience."

*The right to work* is coupled with the prohibition of unemployment, for it is also a duty to work. Beggary is forbidden in Islam. If a person is completely unable to earn a living the community has to provide for him. The Prophet said: "It is better to collect wood and sell it, than to seek charity." 'Umar said: "No one should be lazy, for the sky does not rain gold and silver."

## Liberty, Fraternity and Equality

It puzzles the Muslim to find that historians in the West date "Liberty, Fraternity and Equality" from the French Revolution. And never a word about Islam!

Freedom is sacred in Islam. The basic freedom is to free oneself from passions and desires. For instance, the main aim of fasting all through the month of Ramaḍān (no food or drink from sunrise to sunset) is to train the individual to be able to say "No" to himself whenever it should be said. This type of freedom is so important that the Prophet likened it to winning a major battle. Returning from a battle, he commented, "We are back from the minor *Jihād* (holy war) to the major *Jihād*," referring to conquering one's moods and passions. And again, "Might is not to be assessed in terms of physical strength. The strong man is he who can control himself when angered."

Freedom from greed is stressed, and freedom from the fear of other mortal men. The Qur'ān is very rich in verses emphasising full regard for God alone. "Fear them not, and fear Me."[3] "Worship God, and let nothing share (worship) with Him."[4] "They fight in the cause of God and they never fear blame from any blamer."[5]

Freedom from the fear of men is much encouraged by the fact that in Islam man's relation with God is a direct one, without intermediary. There are no clergy in Islam and all are equal in the eyes of God. The Qur'ān stresses this direct relationship: "When those who worship Me ask you concerning Me, I am indeed close to them. I listen to the prayer of every suppliant when he calls on Me. Let them also with a will listen to My call, and believe in Me, that they may walk in the right way."[6]

Other aspects of freedom were stressed by Islam fourteen centuries ago. Freedom of religious belief is expressed in the Qur'ān. "Let there be no compulsion in religion. Truth stands out clear from error."[7] Personal security and freedom from unlawful arrest are established Islamic rules. The second caliph 'Umar, for example, was unable to prosecute people caught drinking (illegally) in their own houses because he had no right of entry. As to equality before the law, and equality of opportunity, there is only one respect in which one person can be considered better than another, and that is in good deeds and the fear of God. "Dearest to God are those that fear Him most," says the Qur'ān.[8]


## Minorities

An Islamic society is not formed of Muslims only, but of Muslims, Christians and Jews living together under the legal system of Islam.

The legal principle applying to Christians and Jews is: "They have the same rights, and owe the same duties (as we do)."

As a religion, Islam does not put itself in an attitude of conflict towards other God-sent religions. The word *Islām* literally means surrender (to God). God's guidance has been sent through a succession of messengers and prophets who are all revered by a Muslim. Islam is thus the last link of a chain. The Qur'ān reads, "Say (O believers) we believe in God and in that which has been transmitted to us, and in that which has been transmitted to Abraham, Isma'īl, Isaac, Jacob and the Tribes; and that which was given to Moses and Jesus; and that which was given to the Prophets from their Lord. We do not discriminate between them and to Him do we surrender."[9]

Muslims and the People of the Book (Christians and Jews, who have their own sacred writings) can eat each others' food, unless it is specifically prohibited, like pig and alcohol.

A Muslim can take a Christian or a Jewess for a wife, and she has the right to stick to her faith. The People of the Book have freedom to worship in churches and synagogues, which are to be protected by the Muslim ruler. They are equal under Islamic law. Yet on legal points specified in their own religions concerning their private affairs (marriage, divorce, inheritance, etcetera) the Islamic law does not apply and they are left to settle these matters according to their own religion. This is an example of preserving the rights of minorities.

Equality is not only in the court room. Minorities also share the benefits of the principles of social security and "welfare state" laid down since the earliest days of Islam. One day the caliph 'Umar saw a blind old man – a Jew – begging. The man told him, "I beg so as to be able to pay the tribute." (The tribute was a tax imposed on non-Muslims, who were exempted from military service.) 'Umar took him by the hand to his own house and gave him what he needed. He sent orders to his treasurer: "Look after people like him. It would not be fair to take from him when he is young and neglect him when he is old." He decreed that old age should be a reason for exemption from the tribute, as well as illness and disablement. On his way to Damascus, 'Umar once encountered a group of Christian lepers, and ordered food and money to be given them.

## The Right of Ownership – Private Property

Private ownership in Islam is a concept radically different from that of either communism or capitalism.

In Islam total ownership is God's.

The right of ownership that has been bestowed on us is secondary to this.

"To God belongeth whatever is in the heavens and the earth."[10] "Give them something yourselves out of the means which God has given you."[11]

The owner of property should realise that he is God's agent. In his capacity as owner, he must behave in accordance with the ways of God.

Indeed, God's ownership extends to the owner himself. Islam pervades all aspects of life, all the time. In the eyes of a Muslim, whatever he does or thinks, while at work or at leisure, be it private or public, personal or social, concealed or revealed, popular or unpopular, is a matter of the relationship between God and himself.

Private ownership in Islam entails a God-owned owner, given the right to own a God-owned property and to exploit it fully in the ways of God. This right of ownership, once assumed, is very strongly protected in Islam. But in its respect for private ownership, Islam does not foster greed or materialism. These are tempered by conscience, and by legal safeguards. For instance, it was conscience, and that ever-vivid mutual relation with God, that induced the third caliph 'Uthmān to give away a caravan full of foodstuffs free, rejecting an offer to sell it at tenfold price, when Medina was struck by famine.

The right of ownership is the rule. Limitations on it are the exception (contrary to communist theory). Ownership in Islam is a social function, and is interpreted in Islamic law as aiming at the welfare of the community. Where the actions of the owner conflict with this welfare he can be restrained: for instance, in cases of mental incapacity, hoarding, abuse of others' rights, injury to the community (such as monopoly), or neglect of the needs of the poor.

A prerequisite of enjoying the right of ownership is recognition of the rights of the needy. The Prophet was heard to say: "He cannot be a believer. He cannot be a believer. He cannot be a believer." When asked "Who?", the Prophet answered: "He who sleeps the night with a full stomach, while his neighbour is hungry." Private ownership is so sacred that in ordinary circumstances a thief might have his hand amputated: but if he proves needy the punishment is suspended. It is the duty of the governor to fulfil this need for food. If the alms tax (zakāt)[12] together with money given for charity do not suffice, the governor must impose heavier taxes on those better off, in favour of the needy.

In times of war or famine resources are to be shared. In a year of famine, 'Umar suggested that each household should double the number of people they were feeding, "for people will not perish of half-empty stomachs."

No individual right or freedom can be regarded in isolation. The Prophet told this story. A group of men shared a ship – some on the upper deck, some on the lower. Whenever they wanted water, those below had to come up.

So they thought it might be a good idea to cut a hole in their part of the vessel so as not to bother the ones above. If those on deck allowed them to do this, the ship would sink and all would be drowned. If they prevented them, all would survive. Whole nations today are faced with similar dilemmas.

## The State: Authority and Responsibility

Islam couples authority with responsibility, as in our day the welfare state sets out to do.

The fourth caliph 'Ali wrote instructions to his viceroy in Egypt: "Fear God in regard to the lowest class in society, who are helpless, poor and miserable. You are responsible to God, for He entrusted them to you. The distant should receive as much as those who are near. Give each his due, and if you think this is beneath your dignity, do not make excuses. You will not be forgiven if you ignore minor matters to concentrate on those which seem important. Look into the affairs of those who are so weak that they cannot reach you. Appoint God-fearing and humble persons to bring their affairs before you. Give attention to the helpless orphans and the young who would never beg. The burden of responsibility on a viceroy is indeed a heavy one."

The caliph Umar ibn Abd el-Aziz said: "If a mule stumbles in Iraq (far away in the empire) I shall find myself responsible to God for it on the day of judgment: why had I not paved the road properly?" There are innumerable examples of this coupling of authority with responsibility. As the Prophet said: "Every one of you is a shepherd and is responsible for his flock. The governor is a shepherd – so is the man with a family, the woman in her household, the servant with his master's money. All these are shepherds, responsible for the flock entrusted to them."

This is a passing glimpse of Islam,
And it has much to offer to our restless world.
But it seems to be an abandoned treasure,
Abandoned by those who bear its name.
No wonder they are so different from the glory I describe,
And unless they go back to it again, they will remain
Lost in bewilderment, at the rear of Humanity's procession.
For it is the remedy, the light and the guidance from God
    For them – and for the world.

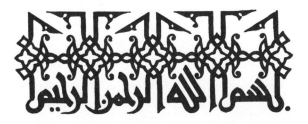

"In the Name of God, Most Gracious, Most Merciful"

# CHAPTER FIVE

# Concepts of Society in the Muslim World

Islam teaches that God is concerned not only with moral and ethical reform, but also with social emancipation and economic conditions.

Abdel Moghny Said[1]

Islam strikes a balance between the two extremes of capitalism and socialism.

Muhammad Qutb[2]

The simultaneous stress on both the material and the spiritual aspects of life is a unique characteristic of the Islamic economic system. This synthesis of the material and the spiritual is what is missing in the other two systems, capitalism and socialism. Both the capitalist and the socialist systems have neglected the spiritual needs of the human personality.

Muhammad Umar Chapra[3]

Contemporary attempts to base the life of nations on Islamic principles cover a wide range. All are profoundly influenced by the example of the Prophet and of the early Muslim community in Medina. They are also strongly influenced by reactions to events and trends in the Western world, both capitalist and communist.

The great adjustments that are taking place in Muslim society are happening at a time when it feels itself under threat from a dominant civilisation which, while no longer politically imperialist, is imposing its norms of behaviour and its materialism on others. Reactions towards the "West" face Muslims with difficult dilemmas.

The search goes on for answers to social and world problems that are consonant with Islamic tradition, neither merely reactions to nor adaptations of alien thought.

"The dominant, permanent factor in Muslim countries," says Dr Fathi Osman, former editor of the *Islamic World Review*, "is Islam as a comprehensive way of life." It is important to realise, he adds, that those who hold this view can be progressive – recognising that not everything "modern" is tied to secularism. The Islamic revival is many-sided, forward-looking as well as traditional.

The tide of renewal in the Muslim world began to flow more than a century ago, with movements such as that of the Wahhabis in Arabia, the Arab awakening in the Near East, and the expansion of Islam south of the Sahara.

The Twentieth Century has seen a war of ideologies – of powerful ideas regarding man and society. Every tide of ideology that has swept through the world during the course of the past decades has had its observers, its critics and sometimes its supporters in the Muslim world. Liberalism and socialism in turn were interpreted in Muslim terms. The atheistic creed of communism has never been acceptable to Muslims, but the Marxist diagnosis of society and history has had its influence in various quarters. Nationalism, though contrary to the Islamic concept of the universal community, the *Ummah*, helped to raise many local and regional loyalties, as well as to inspire the larger vision of Pan-Arabism. Young men – and women also – of each succeeding generation pinned their hopes of radical change to one banner or another: often to suffer disillusionment when the promises of their leaders were not fulfilled.

More and more, hopes of profound change on a national and global scale came to focus on a return to the teachings of Islam. Islam itself could be viewed as an ideology, in the sense of a comprehensive system of ideas that embraces the whole of life.

Some of many trains of thought and action are indicated here: a view on Arab Socialism; the principles of Islamic banking by one of its pioneers; an insight into the universal nature of science; and how the West is seen. Is it irretrievably decadent, or are its people possible partners in fashioning a new age? The key to all progress is in the renewal of faith.

"Three things strengthen a nation's defences:
gentleness, justice, and generosity"

# Origins of Arab Socialism

The Islamic principles on which Arab socialism was based differ fundamentally from dialectical materialism.

One of those who contributed to the development of independent Arab socialist thinking is Abdel Moghny Said, until 1975 Under-Secretary in the Ministry of Manpower, Cairo. He is known for his pioneering work in the field of workers' education. In his book, *Arab Socialism*,[4] he traces its origins in the thought and practice of the Qur'ān and the Prophet.

> The concept of Arab socialism actually existed for many centuries before modern Arab nationalism came upon the scene. Its roots were planted long before Marx. They lie deep in the soil of Islam and in the cultural heritage of the Arabs.

> All the great monotheistic religions were cradled in these Eastern Mediterranean lands which have always been the home of the Arab people. The impulse towards social emancipation is found in all these religions, but it is perhaps most developed in the precepts of Islam. The Qur'ān makes it clear that, as well as setting up moral standards as a basis of decent behaviour and better human relations, religions must bring help to the poor and improve the living standards of the masses. In previous revelations the message was simple: "Do not exploit; be charitable; practise unselfishness." In Islam, for the first time, an economic theory of equal opportunities and fair distribution was outlined.

> Without being too theological, it is possible to explore the social and economic implications of Islam and the principles which have influenced contemporary Arab socialist thought . . . Islam teaches that God is concerned not only with moral and ethical reform, but also with social emancipation and economic conditions.

> The Qur'ān provides a basis for a moral interpretation of history; an interpretation which is deeper and broader than that of Karl Marx because it covers both the moral and material aspects, while that of Marx concentrates entirely on the material aspects, being greatly influenced by the materialistic evolutionary philosophies of his time. Religion is not the opium of the people. The great religions aimed at a classless society, where equality, justice and prosperity would prevail. In their principles, and particularly in Islam, which Marx completely ignored, we can trace much that pointed towards socialism.[4]

# A New Economic Order

Muslims responsible for the policy of nations – Asian and African as well as Arab – see the teachings of the Qur'ān as having relevance to major questions of economics, and also to the stewardship of money and the distribution of world resources.

Banking is one field where practices based on these teachings have been increasingly explored and expanded. In the 1970's and 1980's numbers of Islamic banks were set up, based on the principles of partnership and the sharing of profit and loss. It is essential that the system should be interest-free, since the Qur'ān specifically forbids usury, and this is generally taken to include any form of interest. But the emphasis is on working out a positive system, not merely on excluding an incentive regarded as wrong. By 1987 there were more than 100 Islamic banks and financial institutions throughout the world, including multi-national banking companies. The Islamic Development Bank (IDB) was established in 1975 by the Organisation of the Islamic Conference (OIC) to undertake long-term financing of development projects.[5]

One of the pioneers of these developments is Prince Mohammed Al-Faisal Al-Saoud, Chairman of the International Association of Islamic Banks. In 1981 he founded the Geneva-based Dar-al-Mal al-Islami (DMI). The aim is that Islamic banks and interest-based banks should view each other not as competitors but as partners. One of many steps towards this goal was a symposium of bankers held in Baden-Baden, West Germany, in May 1981, organised by the Syma Institute and chaired by Prince Mohammed.

In his inaugural address he outlines some value premises of Islam. (1) The unity (*tawḥīd*) of thought under God: His power and direction are relevant to every aspect of life. (2) The vice-gerency of man who is God's deputy and who has to act as a trustee: with no extravagance, no waste, but positive utilisation of the available resources. (3) The search for justice, political and social as well as individual. From such a value-framework, he says, the economist will derive a new set of policy conclusions. The thrust of economic analysis will move from what people demand, to what the world needs, and this will be a revolutionary change in economic thinking.

The basic principles of Islamic banking and finance are not new. What is new is only in the application. Our philosophy is based on the Qur'ān in which there are certain things that are given, things which

49

do not bear discussion, because we cannot in any way adjust them. However, there is a wide area in which innovation, new approaches and methods can be applied. We feel we can contribute to the solution of some of the problems in the economies of the world today. We are trying to help in relieving the pressures on the Third World by mobilizing the resources of the Islamic countries through Islamic banking.

Man has been created as God's surrogate in this world. Therefore he is not a totally free agent in his social and economic interactions. There is a certain code. The question of interest is one thing, but more important is the total integration of morality in the dealings of any human being in any endeavour he undertakes.

Economics, as we understand it in its classical form, is the satisfaction of the need for goods and services. With Islam, the definition is slightly different. It is the material satisfaction of the need of society according to the role man plays in this world. This entails certain limitations, which make it different from the western concept of total freedom of action.

Trusteeship brings the idea of accountability in this world before humans, and before God in the life hereafter . . . We shall have to develop social accounting over against the type of accounting with which we are familiar at the moment . . . These concepts are not just ethical norms, but have important economic consequences.

In this new approach, we do not claim that we have all the answers or that we have been able to develop all the solutions. We would like to learn from other traditions, and we would like to see others also adopt a more open attitude to the study of the Muslim approach to economics.[6]

# Science and Faith

The search for knowledge is a duty in Islam. European scholarship owes a debt to the Muslim world for its earlier leadership in the scientific field. Now, however, "The Muslim World can and should learn from and profit by the West, particularly in the spheres of modern sciences and technology." Muhammad Asad, author of *The Road to Mecca*, is one among many who develop this theme.

Never have the worlds of Islam and the West come so close to one another as today. Cultural imitation, opposed to creativeness, is bound to make a people small . . . Not that the Muslims could not learn much from the West, especially in the fields of science and technology. But the acquisition of scientific notions and methods is not really "imitation"; and certainly not in the case of a people whose faith commands them to search for knowledge wherever it is to be found. Science is neither Western nor Eastern, for all scientific discoveries are only links in an unending chain of intellectual endeavour which embraces mankind as a whole.

Every scientist builds on the foundations supplied by his predecessors, be they of his own nation or of another; and this process of building, correcting and improving goes on and on, from man to man, from age to age, from civilisation to civilisation, so that the scientific achievements of a particular age or civilisation can never be said to "belong to that age or civilisation." At various times one nation, more vigorous than others, is able to contribute more to the general fund of knowledge; but in the long run the process is shared, and legitimately so, by all. There was a time when the civilisation of the Muslims was more vigorous than the civilisation of Europe. It transmitted to Europe many technological inventions of a revolutionary nature, and more than that: the very principles of that 'scientific method' on which modern science and civilisation are built. Nevertheless, Jabir ibn Hayyan's fundamental discoveries in chemistry did not make chemistry an "Arabian" science; nor can algebra and trigonometry be described as "Muslim" sciences, although the one was evolved by Al-Khwarizmi and the other by Al-Battani, both of whom were Muslims: just as one cannot speak of an "English" theory of Gravity, although the man who formulated it was an Englishman. All such achievements are the common property of the human race. If, therefore, the Muslims adopt, as adopt they must, modern methods in science and technology they will do no more than follow the evolutionary instinct which causes men to avail themselves of other men's experiences.[7]

# Change Through Renewal

The Islamic concept of change in society is renewal (*tajdīd*), as the key to reform (*iṣlāḥ*).

> The Prophet did not start with a system, or with large numbers. He began with change in the hearts of men and women – his wife, his closest friends. The idea of reform is not the modern one, which begins with the outward, trying to reform the world but never man himself.[8]

Africa south of the Sahara has seen a vigorous expansion of Islam during the nineteenth and twentieth centuries. This renewal of Islam in West Africa may be regarded as "a model of *tajdīd*", suggests Dr A. R. Doi, Director of the Center for Legal Studies, Ahmadu Bello University, Zaria.[9] The revered Shehu (Shaikh) Usumanu Dan Fodio (d. 1817), scholar and preacher in what is now Northern Nigeria, was regarded by his thousands of followers as the Renewer (*mujaddid*) of his age. In one of his many books he speaks of the character of such a reformer.

> It is related [in a saying of the Prophet] that at the beginning of every century God will send a learned man to the people to renew their faith. The characteristics of this man must be that he commands what is right and forbids what is disapproved of, that he reforms the affairs of the people, and judges between them, and that he assists the truth against vanity and the oppressed against the oppressors, in contrast to the characteristics of the other learned men of his age.[10]

The struggle the Shehu declared against rulers he regarded as corrupt began with preaching (the *jihād* of the word). At the risk of his life he took a stand against an injustice, and his struggle turned into an open revolt (the *jihād* of the sword). With his brother Abdullahi and his son Muhammadu Bello he established a state in the new city of Sokoto. This became the centre of a renaissance of poetry, literature and religious study, as well as of prosperous trade. All three were learned and scholarly men: more than a hundred books by them survive. These were concerned with the application of the precepts of Islam to the practical affairs of home, trade and state, and also with the poems, in Arabic and in the vernacular languages, which helped to make the teachings of Islam live for a population largely illiterate. The memory of Usumanu Dan Fodio is still a powerful influence among the more than 150 million Muslims in West African countries, and also in the Sudan.

Renewal in this spirit is the aim of the Emir of Kano, HH Alhaji Ado Bayero. He sees his responsibilities as extending to the contribution a united Nigeria can make to the world. At the end of Ramadan 1988 he invited chiefs from the south of Nigeria, as well as his northern neighbours, to celebrate the Feast, the 'Id al-fiṭr. Together with the Anglican Bishop of Kano, he spoke of uniting peoples of all creeds on the firm ground of moral rectitude, selflessness, and dedication for the betterment of mankind. In a situation tense with recent religious conflict, he and the Bishop gave joint witness to "religion as an agent of unity rather than of division and destruction." Amid the blare of trumpets and the thunder of hooves as thousands of horsemen thronged the ancient city, a note was sounded of quiet faith for the future.[11]

Hausa motifs
Northern Nigeria

# Islam and the West

Over the past hundred years, a renewal of faith and confidence has come to the Muslim world. The forms of this renewal have been manifold: its expressions range from the personal to the running of states, from individual integrity to steps towards a new economic order, from scientific research to art and poetry.

The springs of renewal, or resurgence, in the Muslim world may be discerned in the Qur'ān, in the potency of its teachings and of the basic tenets of Islam. What actually occasioned it, at this time in history, was reaction to the domination of western civilisation, in its political form of imperialism and, more insidiously, in the onslaught of its materialism and secularism.

A reaction had to come. Revulsion against the West was inevitable, and might take controversial forms – not always viewed by Muslims as true to the best in Islam. It was not a reaction against Christianity, but against moral corruption as well as economic and political domination.

In face of the threat of a dominant culture, three possible courses present themselves: rejection, surrender or a selective choice, says Sayyid Abul Hasan Ali Nadwi, Rector of the Nadwat al-Ulama Islamic University in Lucknow. One of the most widely read authors of his time, he has written more than 40 books – in Arabic, Urdu and English. His insights into the world situation and the demands it makes on Muslims have done much to challenge the fears and raise the hopes, especially of the younger generation.

In his book, *Western Civilisation – Islam and Muslims*, he analyses the choices that face them.

> An unrelenting battle of ideas and ideals is taking place throughout the Muslim world – a clash between the Islamic and the Western concepts of life, values and traditions. The past history of the Islamic countries, the indestructible attachment of the Muslim masses everywhere to Islam, the ideals which inspired them in their struggle for freedom – all these things demand that Islamic values alone should have a claim on their leadership. On the other hand, the intellectual make-up, education and political interests of the ruling classes in Muslim countries require that Western forms of life should be pushed forward.
>
> The attitude of rejection and withdrawal is emphatically futile. It is bound to fail. No nation can aspire to maintain its individuality which

lacks faith in itself and is plagued with an inferiority complex. All its efforts to hold its ground against a mighty civilisation, which has also become the dominant trend of the time, must ultimately fail.

In contrast there is the philosophy of defeatism, capitulation, servility. Its advocates are ardent, though immature, disciples of the West. Modernism to them means westernisation.

A man who does not make the West his preceptor and relegate himself to the rank of a pupil, but treats it as an associate, [can] make his own contribution. He ought to know that if he has to learn a great deal from the West, the West too has to learn no less from him. His endeavour should be to bring about a synthesis between the material and spiritual forces of the West and East and then to evolve from it a way of life the West may also be compelled to adopt, and which may serve as an inspiration to the most highly advanced nations of the present day world.[12]

## "Arousing the Conscience of the West"

Criticism of western ways does not necessarily regard the fight for values as confined to the Muslim world, nor as irretrievably lost in western society. Dr. Fathi Osman, former editor of the *Islamic World Review*, in a seminar held at the Oxford Centre for Islamic Studies (February 1987), gave points of common hope and advance, providing grounds for co-operation. As the shadow of colonialism recedes, he said, new friendships are arising. Business relationships enable economic problems to be tackled together. And above all within the structure of western society there are many positive initiatives, "arousing the conscience of the West and countering the impression of an imminent collapse of standards and values."

Response to such initiatives of change, recognised in the conduct of Christians encountered in the West, was confirmed by a Muslim Brother from the Sudan. "I have moved from condemnation to the realisation that there are people we can and should work with," he said. "Absolute moral standards provide the area of co-operation to achieve the Will of God."

# CHAPTER SIX

## *Family Life*

The family is a divinely-inspired institution that came into existence with the creation of man. The human race is a product of this institution and not the other way round.

Khurshid Ahmad[1]

Woman must be regarded as equal to man and must shed the remaining shackles that impede her from taking a constructive part in life.

The family is the primary cell in society, and as such it must be afforded every protection in the national interest.

Abdel Moghny Said[2]

Of all the questions that exercise the minds of Muslims, those connected with family life are the most sensitive. Muslims are proud of their traditions, and wish to maintain them. Western culture with its permissive standards has an impact on their sons and daughters which they see as a threat to their whole way of life. Advance in technology is regarded as essential: but there is widespread fear of the retrogression in character that often seems to accompany it.

Certain practices are an essential part of religion. Others are a matter of custom, and can be set aside. Every Muslim community is in process of some degree of adjustment in regard to the position of women, to marriage customs and to relations between the generations.

These dilemmas are reflected in what Muslims say about their family life. But in comparison with the ever-increasing rate of marital breakdown in the Western world they understandably feel that they have something of value not only to preserve, but to offer. Mr Khurshid Ahmad, Chairman of the Islamic Foundation, Leicester, writing on "Family Life in Islam", says, "It is the family that provides the most congenial climate for the development and fulfilment of human personality."[3] Marriage and the family in Islam should be studied in the context of the scheme of life Islam wants to establish. "We refuse to accept the value-neutral approach that willy-nilly fashions the life and perspectives of man in the secular culture of the West today. We think the disintegration of the family in the West is, in part, a result of confusion about the place and the role of the family in society and about the purpose of life itself."[4]

About a third of the legal injunctions in the Qur'ān deal with family matters, and with the network of rights and obligations that provide the basis for family life. These aim to produce the attitudes and behaviour patterns that Islam wants to foster in society. The Muslim family is an extended family, normally with three or four generations within its circle. Marriage in Islam is not a temporary union and is meant to last for life. Dissolution of marriage is, however, permitted if it has irretrievably broken down: but before divorce the law demands an attempt at reconciliation by the families concerned. "The natural prevalence of monogamy as the normal type of sexual relationship" is more and more the practice in Muslim countries. Nevertheless, a limited polygamy is seen as a realistic need in certain circumstances: and indeed as preferable to the "concealed polygamy" without responsibility, in some ways tolerated in Western society. "Islam is a practical religion and is meant for the guidance of human beings made of flesh and bones."[5] The ideal is a loving, stable family in which the best of human nature can flower.

# An Arab Family

A Muslim lawyer, Mr Jamil Nasir, head of an Arab family in Jerusalem, made the following observations on the social traditions of Arab family life. In 1966, his daughter invited me to spend an evening in her home. She was then Vice-Principal of a Teacher Training College, and had just returned from a course in "counselling" in the United States. She is one of ten children, who include two medical doctors and a Ph.D. Three of her sisters were living at home: two of them principals of schools, and the youngest a teacher. Present also was an Irish sister-in-law, whose doctor husband had refused better paid posts so as to continue to work in Jerusalem.

Awkward questions arise as one sits in such homes. "What is happening to your life in America, in Britain?" "What about these attacks on old people for their money?" "Why do you let young people treat your lovely parks as bedrooms?" On this particular evening, the conversation turned on a tragic event. In London, the sons of a mutual friend had been attacked in the street. One had lost an eye and was in a serious condition.

My friend's father, the lawyer, said: "How can these things happen in a civilised country? Here, the police find and punish thieves within a few days. In your cities, I hear, they cannot find them. Our young men feel responsible to their families. They are more afraid of what the family would do or say than they would be of the police."

I asked him to tell me more about the ties which bind Arab families, and which, he said, still implant a sense of privilege and responsibility in each member, young and old. He said:

Arab social life is based on ancient traditions, and on the teaching of the Qur'ān. The individual is responsible to the family, and the family to the tribe or community. If an individual commits wrong, the family and community will be held responsible: and if wrong is done to an individual his family and community automatically support him.

Thus an individual is very cautious in his dealings and behaviour, because he will be subject to reprimand by his relatives and his community, all of whom he will have involved by his wrongdoing. The reputation of the individual man or woman reflects on his family and community, and they have to pay any fine he incurs.

From an early age, children are taught not to cause any inconvenience to parents and relatives by bad behaviour. They grow up in this spirit, and there is therefore hardly any juvenile crime, theft or injury committed. They learn to respect older people, to help their neighbours and to be generous to guests. Thus we find a high level of security in Arab countries.

When a man marries, he remains closely connected with his father and mother, sisters and grandparents. Together they share happiness and sorrow, and meet the events and accidents of life, and take the lawful and customary procedures if their rights are infringed. If necessary, all the relatives will act together. Marriage and funeral expenses are corporate responsibilities.

Girls are treated equally with boys, and every man is obliged to protect his women relatives as far back as the connections of the "fourth grandfather". A woman after marriage retains her father's family name, rather than taking that of her husband, as an indication that her father is responsible for her all her life. Her parents must visit her during every big holiday season, and take her a present. Thus she feels the strength and protection of her male relatives. This encourages her, and if she gets into difficulties it helps to deter her from wrong-doing.

There are customary procedures to be followed, as well as legal ones, if something goes wrong between families. For example, news came that my son had been involved in a car accident in Amman. While he was driving, a boy was knocked down. The police completely exonerated the driver, but this was not the point as far as the family was concerned. We went straight to Amman, found three respected men of standing, and sent them to the boy's family to arrange a week's truce between the families. (Among the Bedouin, if someone is killed and such a truce is not quickly settled, a life will be taken to restore the family honour.) The boy was lying in hospital with concussion. After a week, the truce was renewed for two months. The boy was unconscious for fifteen days. If he had died, we would have had to pay the sum enjoined by the Prophet Muḥammad to be paid for an accidental death, now reckoned as £350. Every one of our family – "until the fourth grandfather" and the cousins connected in this degree – would have been liable to contribute. But, thank God, the boy recovered. When the two months were over, there was a ceremony. A sheep was killed and many members of both families were present at the feast. "Thank God, the boy is well," we said. "We forgive you and realise it was an accident," they said. Peace was restored, and documents signed to say so.

The father is responsible for his sons and his daughters. If a girl does something wrong with a man, the family honour is at stake. There are cases when the brother kills her, or kills the man who wronged her. The law takes into consideration "defence of life, property and honour," and a lenient sentence may be given: three years' or seven years' imprisonment, rather than hanging.

Hospitality is another side of Arab tradition. There still exists the custom among Arab chiefs of generously welcoming a guest for three days before asking him his name and the purpose of his visit. Then he is offered any help he needs.

Mutual assistance and co-operation; help for the poor and needy; respect for others' faith and rights as well as safeguarding one's own; obedience to law and custom; the inclination to treat others as one wishes others to treat oneself: all these are part of the Arab attitude and way of life.

Jamil Nasir, Jerusalem[6]

Early mosaics: olive and almond trees
Dome of the Rock, Jerusalem, 7th century AD

# The Position of Women

The traditional place of women in Islam is a high one. Modern writers all stress the improvements the Prophet Muḥammad brought about in their position and rights. Undue restrictions prevalent at certain periods of history have been, it is said, a matter of social custom, not of religion itself.

## Equal – and Different

According to the Qur'ān, women are equal to men as human beings – different in their role. In the presence of their Creator, their basic duties are the same. Daily prayer, fasting and pilgrimage are incumbent on them. They are alike in their hopes of paradise and certainty of judgment.

> Men who surrender unto Allah,
>     And women who surrender,
> and men who believe,
>     And women who believe,
> And men who speak the truth,
>     And women who speak the truth,
> And men who presevere in righteousness,
>     And women who presevere,
> And men who are humble,
>     And women who are humble,
> And men who give alms,
>     And women who give alms,
> And men who fast,
>     And women who fast,
> And men who guard their modesty,
>     And women who guard their modesty,
> And men who make mention of Allah much,
>     And women who make mention of Him –
> Allah hath prepared for them forgiveness and a vast reward.
>
> Qur'ān: Sūra 33:35 The Clans

> If any do deeds of righteousness – be they male or
> female – and have faith, they will enter paradise.
>
> Qur'ān: Sūra 4:124 Women

Women have the right to own property, and to inherit it, and to run their own businesses. It is often pointed out that these measures of equality were only won in western society in the Nineteenth Century, whereas they have existed in Muslim law since the time of the Prophet.

At the same time, men have duties towards the women of the family. A wife must be maintained by her husband, even if she has means of her own. This is used to explain the inequality of inheritance – a man receives a larger share of a family legacy than does a woman.

## Women in History

Women played an important part in the early days of the Prophet's mission and the coming of Islam. His wife Khadija – a business woman in her own right – was the first to support him in his calling. In their home in Mecca their daughter Fatima and her sisters grew up. After Khadija's death, and his move to Medina, much of our knowledge of what he said and what he did is owed to the loving insight and acute perception of his young wife Aisha. These three names are very often given to Muslim girls.

In seeking their role in society, today's Fatimas, Khadijas and Aishas have the example of these early pioneers of Islam, and also of many others who played their part later in the flowerings of Islamic life and civilisation. In every age some outstanding women make their mark.

Many saintly women are recorded, among them Rābi'a al-Adawiyya, whose life of poverty in Basra challenged the rich and powerful in the early days of the Abbasid empire. The great philosopher and mystic Al-Ghazali quoted what he learned from her about the love of God, and her prayers still sift the motives of those who use them.

Oh my Lord, the stars are shining and the eyes of men are closed and every lover is alone with his beloved, and here I am alone with Thee.

Oh God, if I worship Thee for fear of hell, burn me in hell,
If I worship Thee in hope of Paradise, exclude me from paradise,
But if I worship Thee for Thine own sake grudge me not Thine everlasting beauty.[7]

In contrast with Rābi'as life of dedication in poverty, many women have been honoured for the use they made of their wealth. One of the most famous of these a generation after Rābi'a was Zubaida, wife and cousin of the caliph Harun al-Rashid. She is still remembered with gratitude by pilgrims to Mecca for the beneficence of her provision of water in the city and along the road from Iraq.[8]

Most women who have wielded influence in Muslim society have done so through their sons. The position of the mother in the family is central, and an often-quoted saying of the Prophet is, "Heaven lies at the feet of a mother."

## Education for Women

The present resurgence of Islam was already gathering momentum at the beginning of this century. Leading thinkers – the Egyptian Muhammad Abdo and the Indian Amir Ali among them – called for the restoration to women of rights given to them in the Qur'ān but often ignored in practice. During the Ottoman period women's education had been almost totally neglected, and in the early 1900's experiments in the education of girls began simultaneously in different parts of the Muslim world. Today, such education is given high priority by the governments of Muslim countries, including Saudi Arabia. Women are graduating from scores of universities, and there is a growing body of skilled professional women: doctors, nurses, teachers, lawyers, also architects and engineers. There are also widespread literacy programmes, reaching the countrywomen.

## Freedom for Service

Many tensions arise in the effort to give maximum service to the community without disrupting the pattern of family life and without losing prized traditions and identity. To understand these tensions it is necessary to take into account the revulsion against elements of decadence in western society. The idea that "progress" lies in imitation of the West is rightly rejected. The excesses of some upholders of "liberation" for women have made it more difficult for women in Muslim countries to pursue their own path towards fuller responsibility. To find the way to this, without eroding the importance of motherhood, or of loyalty to Islam, is the challenge this generation is facing.

Two quotations show these concerns from very different points of view. The first comes from a woman who has held cabinet office in Jordan, the second from a Shi'ite scholar in Iran.

Mrs Inam Mufti was appointed Minister for Social Affairs in Jordan in January 1980. She was formerly Principal of the UNRWA Women's Vocational College, Ramallah, in the West Bank. She has been a pioneer of education in many forms, and in the 1940's was herself one of the first girls to go to college from her home town in Safad, in Northern Palestine. She is concerned with what women will bring with them into public life, with questions of values as well as of skills. Women, she thinks, can bring into every branch of a nation's work a

63

sense of service and a care for individuals. As they do so, they will become pace-setters for standards of excellence and integrity.

We want to find a balanced formula for partnership which takes into consideration all the responsibilities of women. The role of the mother in the community must never be underestimated. But apart from women with young children, there are many who do not find full employment and expression in their homes. Here is a potential that the nation cannot afford to neglect.

Certain old attitudes and prejudices must change, and they are changing. In the past, these have limited the activities of women, and their freedom of expression. But there is nothing in the true tradition of Islam to hold women back. The Qur'ān says that every man and woman must search for knowledge, and also tells them to engage in honest work.

We need to move with caution so as not to lose the family life we prize. We do not want to find ourselves neglecting either our children or our old people. There is a give and take between the generations, a mutual interplay of service and responsibility, which we must maintain. The preparation of women citizens must be personal, as well as vocational. They bring up the men, and character building for the future is their most vital role.[9]

Sayid Mujtaba Musawi Lari is the son and grandson of respected Shi'ite scholars in Iran. His grandfather was one of those instrumental in bringing into being the Iranian constitution of 1906. He himself studied theology for ten years in the city of Qum, an ancient centre of religious training not far from Tehran. He then spent some time in Germany for health reasons. His shrewd observations and wide reading during this period of ill health formed the basis of a book *Western Civilisation through Muslim Eyes*.[10]

He portrays the inconsistencies, the absurdities, alongside the arrogance, which he finds in western society. The workless, the hungry, the lonely old and the delinquent young, the pampered dogs and battered wives, for him mirror the callousness of a society which appears to have lost its heart and soul. If the picture is overdrawn, it is nevertheless a genuine expression of views widely held. It makes it understandable that western strictures on other societies are not better received.

To his picture of the West he adds his own reflections on Islam's contribution to the solution of social problems. In a chapter on the family he speaks of marriage, and the importance of "steering the life-force into its God-given legitimate channels where peace of mind and calm of conscience accompany the happiness of a shared life."

Modern disrespect for the bond of marriage is due to the neglect of this high conception of wedlock. It has been degraded by a mass of petty dreams and twisted imaginations. Men's thinking about marriage was in ruins before their families began to fall apart.

On the position of women Sayid Musawi Lari writes:

The West's vociferous partisans of Women's Lib have no idea of the revolutionary leap forward in women's position which Islam brought about. Islam regards both man and woman as created by God to rise to the full stature of the perfect human. Each is a precious soul. They are complementary to each other. Many women possess such personal excellences and intelligence that they attain great heights of true humanity and happiness. Many men, alas, fall to the lowest depths because they flout reason and abandon themselves to their passions.

A woman, he says, tackled the formidable caliph 'Umar on a legal point in public. 'Umar could not deny the accusation and said, "It was a man who erred and a woman who uttered the truth." He contrasts the property rights of the Muslim woman with the legal position of women in Europe until recent years, quoting the Sūra of Women (4: 33) "Whatsoever a man earns is his own. Whatsoever a woman earns is her own." He continues:

It is true that today far too many women are condemned in the East to an unsatisfactory way of life. But this is not due to Islam's regulations. It is due to the neglect of religious precept in political, social and financial institutions.

Poverty is one important reason for the bad conditions under which Eastern women have to live. A few are too rich; but the majority far too poor, victims of hunger and wretchedness. The resultant weakness has deprived people of the strength to rise up and insist on a change in their environment, for the sake of their families and their children. Nor have the women the power in such a situation to make use of their legal rights and to take men to court for the violence and tyranny of their behaviour. Women fear the difficulties of having to live without a male companion in a man's world.

Economic needs cause a diminution in morals and in human affections. Violence and injustice replace moral values.

Although Islamic lands are amongst the worst sufferers from these modern disasters, it is not Islam itself, but the deliberate neglect and abandonment of Islamic principles by Muslims and their leaders which has brought these tragedies upon us. For Islam is the very acme of the counterforces to poverty and injustice, and insists that wealth must be fairly divided amongst people of all classes, declaring that it is wrong for people to have to live under the torture of indigence and its pressure on hearts and souls, not least those of women and children.

Have we not men wise and just enough to eradicate these wrongs? To cure the bitterness which they produce? To re-enact sound Islamic measures? To restore respect for the dictates of piety and reverence for God and men? Should not the same Islam which once rescued woman from degrading depression, now raise her again by instituting a new society?[10]

## The Veil

"The true veil is in the eyes of the men," runs a saying of the Prophet. Women on pilgrimage are not allowed to veil their faces. What is clearly commanded in the Qur'ān is a modesty of dress and behaviour – for both men and women.

The relevant passages are as follows:

Tell the believing men to lower their gaze and be modest. That is purer for them. Lo! Allah is Aware of what they do. And tell the believing women to lower their gaze and be modest, and to display of their adornment only that which is apparent, and to draw their veils over their bosoms, and not to reveal their adornment save to their own husbands or fathers or husband's fathers, or their sons or their husband's sons or their brothers or their brother's sons ... and turn unto Allah together, Oh believers, in order that ye may succeed.

Qur'ān 24:30–31 Light

Oh Prophet! Tell thy wives and thy daughters and the women of the believers to draw their cloaks close round them when they go abroad. That will be better, that so they may be recognised and not annoyed.

Qur'ān 33: 59 The Clans

The commentator Abdullah Yusuf Ali says in notes on these two passages, "The rule of modesty applies to men as well as to women." "The times were those of insecurity, and the women were asked to cover themselves when walking abroad. It was never contemplated that they should be confined to their houses like prisoners." "The object was not to restrict the liberty of women, but to protect them from harm and molestation under the conditions then existing in Medina."[11]

The covering of the face by a veil has never been universal in the Muslim world. Country women go to the fields without a veil, women in some parts of the Muslim world have not adopted it, others during the last decades have discarded it. But the Quranic injunction to modesty, however it is applied, cannot be set aside. Its interpretation has varied, and does vary, but its importance is basic. One interpretation of what constitutes modesty is the long skirt and head scarf worn by many young women – a stricter interpretation than that of some of their mothers.

Some Muslim women note an obsession among western observers with the question of the veil, an emphasis that tends to trivialise an important debate. The point at issue in the many discussions on the subject of women's role and women's dress is not the veil itself, but the values which Muslim society treasures and seeks to maintain. High among these are honour and good faith, pre-marital chastity and fidelity in marriage. "If the veil still exists, it is because those who are wearing it feel it is part of their tradition and part of their lives," says one woman lawyer.[12]

Asked about the question of the veil, a western-educated Iranian woman student said:

> I think the profound reason for the veil in Islam is that a woman should not draw the attention of others. But if deeply inside her aim *is* to draw attention to herself she will do so even by being covered. Therefore it is a question of motive. If our motive is to gain the respect of others we will do this through the way we are: our behaviour, our acts, our thoughts, what we say and what we wear.
>
> A woman can be a centre of attention or she can decide to give attention to others. She can be a cause of crime or a cause of creation. It depends on her deep motives.
>
> Today we talk a lot about "la femme objet", the woman as a material object and not a real human being. And we often blame men for this attitude. They may deserve part of the blame, I do not know. But we are the real cause. We must be able to attract through our naturalness, our freedom from jealousy, hate and selfishness, and through what we think. Dressing in an extravagant fashion must not be the test of being

charming and attractive. We can change such values by rethinking our role and our place in society and the world.[13]

## The Prophet's Marriages

On the Prophet's own family life, the following comment comes from Professor Seyyed Hossein Nasr, author of *Ideals and Realities of Islam, Man and Nature*, and other works:

> During the period of youth when the passions are most strong the Prophet lived with only one wife, who was much older than he, and he also underwent long periods of abstinence. And as a prophet many of his marriages were political ones, which, in the prevalent social structure of Arabia, guaranteed the consolidation of the newly founded community . . . The multiple marriages of the Prophet, far from pointing to his weakness towards "the flesh", symbolise his patriarchal nature and his function, not as a saint who withdraws from the world, but as one who sanctifies the very life of the world by living in it and accepting it with the aim of integrating it into a higher order of reality.
>
> Seyyed Hossein Nasr[14]

## The Origins of Muslim Marriage

The fourth chapter of the Qur'ān is called *Women*, because it deals largely with women's rights. It begins:

> O Mankind! Be careful of your duty to your Lord Who created you from a single soul and from it created its mate and from them twain hath spread abroad a multitude of men and women.

It goes on to urge respect for mothers and for the rights of orphans, then continues:

> Marry of the women who seem good to you two or three or four; and if ye fear that ye cannot do justice (to them) then one (only) . . . Thus it is more likely that ye will not do injustice.[15]

The trend today is to interpret this as a clear discouragement of polygamy. One man commented, "The Qur'ān tells us, 'Marry more than one if you can be fair to them – but you never will be fair.' The

Prophet for certain special reasons married more than one wife and treated them justly. But how can we disregard the word of God in the Qur'ān telling us that we shall not act justly?"

The origins of Muslim marriage, and the special circumstances in which arose its permission of a limited polygamy are explained in *A Muslim Commentary on the Declaration of Human Rights*. The author is Sultanhussein Tabandeh, leader of the Ne'matullahi Sultanalishahi Sufi Order, Iran.

A glance at the situation in the Arab communities of the Pre-Islamic Times of Ignorance reveals how much Islam in fact advanced women's status and improved the conditions of their life.

The enemies of the Muslims attacked them with military force and in the ensuing battles so many men perished that great numbers of women were left without a protector, an almost impossible situation in the desert society of the Arabia of those days. It was to ensure the safety of women bereaved ... that the Prophet was told to grant permission to the Companions each to take one of the bereaved women with her children under his aegis as part of his own family ... and so to extend to the solitary women the assurance of protection and family life.

The new religion at once set to work to purge society of abuses. The imposition of a strict limit of four on the numbers of marriages allowable was one of the first beneficent new regulations.

The legalising of the number of four wives was not a command to take four wives. It was not an order but a limit. This permission is hedged about with many conditions. For instance, the man's finances must be sufficient, his circumstances favour a multiple establishment. His intention must be to be absolutely fair to each wife, his companionship and provision for each be equally shared.

If polygamy is not allowed, circumstances may arise which cause difficulty, sin, confusion or unnecessary strain ... Many reasons make polygamy sensible, reasonable and right. But if a man's motive is merely to satisfy his carnal lusts, polygamy is frowned on, since men are commanded to allow their reason to control their passions. The acceptance of this inner discipline increases the intellectual powers and diminishes the force of fleshly desire.

Sultanhussein Tabandeh[16]

## Marriage in Law

An eminent Indian lawyer, A. A. A. Fyzee, discusses the legal aspect of marriage in his authoritative text book, *Outlines of Muhammadan Law*:

> Marriage, in its legal aspect, is a contract and not a sacrament. There can be no marriage without consent.
>
> In its social aspect, three important factors must be remembered.
>
> (i) Islamic law gives to the woman a definitely high status after marriage.
>
> (ii) Restrictions are placed upon the unlimited polygamy of pre-Islamic times.
>
> (iii) The Prophet, both by example and precept, encouraged the status of marriage. He positively enjoined marriage for all those who could afford it. And the well-known saying attributed to the Prophet, "There is no monkery in Islam", expresses his attitude to celibacy briefly and adequately.
>
> In its religious aspect . . . marriage is recognised in Islam as the basis of society. It is a contract, but it is also a sacred covenant. Marriage as an institution leads to the uplift of man and is a means for the continuance of the human race. Spouses are strictly enjoined to love and honour each other.
>
> Muslim law permits polygamy but does not encourage it, and the Qur'ānic injunction (Sūra 4: 3) shows that in practice perfect equality of treatment on the part of the husband is, for all practical purposes, impossible of achievement. Hence Muslim law as enforced in India has considered polygamy as an institution to be tolerated but not encouraged.

Asaf A. A. Fyzee[17]

# Divorce

There are strict rules and safeguards in the Qur'ān in regard to divorce. Abdel Moghny Said discusses these in his book, *Islam - A Progressive Faith for a Dynamic World*:

Marriage is a noble communion between man and woman, a communion which is blessed by Allah and based on freedom of choice. It is to be made or dissolved by the free consent of both parties.

Islam leaves room for divorce as an undesirability, but not as a right to be excessively used. If it is deemed impossible for a couple to live together, after exhausting all means of conciliation and arbitration, they have but to separate. "If you fear a breach between the two of them, appoint an arbiter from his folk and an arbiter from her folk. If they desire amendment Allah will make them of one mind." (Qur'ān Sūra 4: 35 *Women*) It is clear that divorce is permitted only as a last resort. As Prophet Muḥammad said, "Divorce is the most hateful to Allah among that which is permitted." When divorce is deemed inevitable it must be carried out in a decent and kind way. "Divorce must be pronounced twice and then (a woman) must be retained in honour or released in kindness." (Qur'ān: Sūra 2: 229 *The Cow*)

We would like to emphasise that humanity has learned through its long experience that divorce is an unavoidable necessity in certain cases. This is why divorce is permitted even in countries whose religion does not allow it. As regards this issue, Islam has proved to be realistic.

Abdel Moghny Said[18]

# Family Planning

Statements by Muslim religious authorities have been sought on the question of the use of contraceptive methods, in view of Family Planning programmes. These statements agree that contraception – but not sterilisation – is permissible under Muslim law:

The use of medicine to prevent pregnancy temporarily is not forbidden by religion, especially if repeated pregnancies weaken the woman due to insufficient intervals for her to rest and regain her health. The Qur'ān says: ". . . Allah desireth for you ease; He desireth not . . . hardship for you . . ." (Sūra 2: 185) ". . . And hath not laid upon you in religion any hardship . . ." (Sūra 22: 78) But the use of medicine to prevent pregnancy absolutely and permanently is forbidden by religion.

The Fatwa Committee, Al Azhar University, March 10 1953[19]

There are genuine traditions which allow methods for restricting procreation, such as coitus interruptus ... A corollary of this is the dispensation for the use of medicine for contraception.

The Grand Mufti of Jordan, December 1964[20]

In his book, *The Lawful and the Prohibited in Islam*, Dr Yusuf Al-Qaradawi, Dean of the Department of Sharia, University of Qatar, says:

The preservation of the human species is unquestionably the primary objective of marriage, and such preservation of the species requires continued reproduction. Accordingly, Islam encourages having many children and has blessed both male and female progeny. However, it allows the Muslim to plan his family due to valid reasons and recognised necessities.

Valid reasons given for the use of contraceptives are: fear that the pregnancy or delivery might endanger the life or health of the mother; fear that the burden of children may straiten the family's circumstances so much that one might do something *ḥaram* (forbidden) to satisfy their needs; fear that the children's health or upbringing might suffer, especially that a new pregnancy might harm a previous suckling child. Dr Qaradawi adds:

Imam Aḥmad bin Ḥanbal [founder of one of the four traditional schools of Islamic Law], is of the opinion that contraception requires the consent of the wife, because she has the right both to sexual enjoyment and to decide whether or not she wants a child. It is reported that 'Umar forbade the practice of coitus interruptus without the consent of the wife. This was, on the part of Islam, a noteworthy step toward establishing the rights of women in an age in which they had no rights.[21]

# Abortion: The Islamic Position

While Islam permits preventing pregnancy for valid reasons, it does not allow doing violence to the pregnancy once it occurs, says Dr Yusuf Al-Qaradawi. However, there is one exceptional situation, he says. If it is reliably established that the continuation of the pregnancy would necessarily result in the death of the mother, then, in accordance with the general principle of the Muslim legal code, that of choosing the lesser of two evils, abortion may be performed.[22]

The Islamic position on abortion is examined by Dr Hassan Hathout, FRCSE, Chief Medical Officer, Maternity Hospital, Kuwait.

In February 1971, a seminar was held in Beirut by the International Planned Parenthood Association, on "Induced Abortion – a Hazard to Public Health". Among divergent views, says Dr Hathout, there was a strong current in favour of abortion, but a new impetus was given to the discussion when Islam's attitude was broached. The need was expressed for a study of Islam's stand on planned parenthood from all angles, and especially in relation to abortion, so as to clarify what Muslim law sanctions and proscribes in regard to it.

Dr Hathout's paper, "Induced Abortion", was presented at a further gathering of the association in Rabat, December 1971. A summary of his argument follows:[23]

> I am no stranger to the subject (of abortion) as I encounter it almost daily as obstetrician and gynaecologist. Quite a sizeable part of my life has been spent in study of the human foetus. And I am a believer in Islam who holds that Islam is and should remain the foundation upon which the life of the Muslim should rest.
>
> History shows that man's civilisation has rested on one unique concept, namely man's control over his passions. Without this, he would not have scaled the heights of moral glory nor would his intelligence have proceeded along the path of scientific research. If man were to give his passions free rein, mankind would become a community bent on self-destruction – a disintegrating civilisation.
>
> Lust today is portrayed as an irresponsible beast. Chastity is held to be unreasonable and unacceptable. In Muslim societies, however (and among Christians living among them), virginity before marriage is practically one hundred per cent. This means it is not beyond the reach of possibility. It might be argued that fear and social pressures contribute largely to this figure. But fear is not – and should not be – the sole reason for chastity. Indeed I have known men who practise

self-restraint not out of fear but out of self-respect and respect to those they love. If you love somebody you should not subject them to possible harm.

When doctor and patient discuss this question, there is always a third party present: the foetus, the newcomer waiting at the door. Perhaps the foetus has the added privilege of having his whole life ahead of him. I have come to know the foetus in its various phases, arriving at the conclusion that the foetus is an individual. I have been unable to draw a line between the foetus as a human and a non-human. I have moreover been unable to draw a line telling me where I would have to feel concern for the foetus and where I would have to disregard it. It is confusing and contradictory to hear those voices loudest in the defence of the illegitimate baby, which were most willing to have sacrificed him a few months before, when he was a foetus *in utero*.

Muslim legal views on abortion were unanimous on some points, varied on others. Some were based on the early medical belief that "quickening of life" took place when movement of the foetus could be felt, about four months after conception. This is not now scientific.

Abortion differs from contraception, being an assault on life and therefore a criminal act. All agree that abortion is a crime after "quickening" has taken place, and blood money is due. Opinions differ as to before "quickening". Ghazāli and others hold it a crime against existing life. But if the mother's life is endangered, the lesser evil is to be allowed and the mother saved. The foetus has the right to inherit – and the right to live. To deprive it of this right is prohibited by religion, unless there are strong grounds. These may be the certainty of danger in the present or immediate future to the mother's life, or the strong probability of the baby being born deformed.

To say that a foetus is "unwanted" is a delusion. We have conducted a survey on a group of women – married – who had demanded abortion. When they were delivered of their babies, we asked each one if she still felt the baby was unwanted. The reply of one and all was in the negative.

# CHAPTER SEVEN

## *Parents and Children*

Show kindness to parents . . .
Lower to them the wing of humility
out of tenderness.

Qur'ān Sūra 17: 23–24 *The Israelites*

The name of Allah is repeated to form this eight-pointed star

# Parents and Children in the Qur'ān

Profound issues of love and obedience often arise between parents and children. An Indian mother and daughter discussed their mutual duties, and a subsequent study of what the Qur'ān has to say on the subject revealed an emphasis somewhat different from what they expected. To parents, the utmost kindness is due: and to God, obedience.

Four well-known passages from the Qur'ān are quoted here, followed by some notes from the commentary of Yusuf Ali:

> Thy Lord commanded, "Worship none but Him, and show kindness to parents. If one or both of them attain old age with thee, never say unto them any word expressive of disgust nor reproach them, but address them with excellent speech. And lower to them the wing of humility out of tenderness. And say, 'My Lord have mercy on them even as they nourished me in my childhood.' "

Qur'ān: Sūra 17: 23–24 *The Israelites*

> We enjoined on man kindness to his parents. But if they strive to make thee associate with Me that of which thou hast no knowledge, then obey them not. Unto Me is your return, and I shall inform you of what you did.

Qur'ān: Sūra 29: 8 *The Spider*

> We have enjoined on man concerning his parents – his mother bears him in weakness and his weaning takes two years – "Give thanks to Me and to thy parents. Unto Me is the final return." ... And if they contend with thee to make thee set up equals with Me concerning which thou hast no knowledge, obey them not. Be a kind companion to them in all worldly affairs: and in spiritual matters follow the way of him who turns to Me. Then unto Me will be your return and I will inform you of what you used to do.

Qur'ān: Sūra 31: 14–15 *Luqman*

> We have enjoined on man to be good to his parents. His mother bears him in pain and brings him forth in pain ... When he comes to maturity he says, "My Lord, make me grateful for Thy favour which Thou hast bestowed upon me and my parents, that I may do such good works as please Thee. And make my seed righteous for me. I do turn to Thee, and truly I am of those who submit to Thee." ... But the one who says to his parents, "Fie on you both! God's promise ... is nothing but tales of the ancients," ... will be utterly lost.

Qur'ān: Sūra 46: 15–18 *The Sandhills*

In his notes on the passages in the Qur'ān dealing with parents and children, Abdullah Yusuf Ali makes the following comments:

In matters of faith and worship even parents have no right to force their children ... Children and parents must all remember that they have to go before God's tribunal, and answer each for his own deeds. In cases where one set of people have lawful authority over another set of people (as in the case of parents and children), and the two differ on important matters like that of Faith, the latter are justified in rejecting authority: the apparent conflict will be solved when the whole truth is revealed to all eyes in the final judgment.

Where the duty to man conflicts with the duty to God, it means that there is something wrong with the human will, and we should obey God rather than man. But even here, it does not mean that we should be arrogant or insolent. To parents and those in authority, we must be kind, considerate and courteous, even when they command things which we should not do and therefore disobedience becomes our highest duty ...

In any apparent conflict of duties our standards should be God's Will, as declared to us by His command. That is the way of those who love God: and their motives in disobedience to parents or human authority, where disobedience is necessary by God's law, is not self-willed rebellion or defiance, but love of God, which means the true love of man in the highest sense of the word. And the reason we should give is: "Both you and I have to return to God; therefore not only must I follow God's Will, but you must command nothing against God's Will."

These conflicts may appear to us strange and puzzling in this life. But in God's presence we shall see their real meaning and significance. It may be that that was one way in which our true mettle could be tested: for it is not easy to disobey and love man at the same time.[1]

# Told to the Children

Teaching children religion is reckoned as one of the most important aspects of family life. This is primarily the responsibility of the parents. Children are taught to pray by the time they are seven, often by older brothers and sisters.

Much of the teaching comes in story form: tales of brave and generous men and women who did great things for their fellow men, or about rich and poor people who are unequal in possessions and yet are equal before God.

"Muslim women have a great responsibility for passing on tradition and culture. So it is important to give the children the right examples. Prophet Muḥammad's life is rich in this way," said one mother. It may be one of the older members of the household – grandmother or even great-grandmother – whose story-telling is unforgettable.

The Prophet's life – his boyhood as an orphan, his honesty in business, his calling, his escapes, his struggles as well as his victories – is told and re-told, as are the lives of other prophets. "After the Prophet," said another mother, "my favourite characters are Virgin Mary and Caliph 'Umar. Girls can learn much from Virgin Mary. They can be pure and virgin till they are married – dedicated in a way as she was."[2]

'Umar, the second successor to Muḥammad, is especially popular. He was not only a warrior, but a father to his people. He used to move about Medina at night, to find out how his poorer subjects were living. One of many tales is of his hearing the cry of a hungry child, and himself fetching and cooking food for the family. His conversion – from violent opposition to Muḥammad – was a dramatic turning point in the early growth of Islam. The story is told here from the Children's Page of *The Islamic Review and Arab Affairs* (Woking, September 1967). It is part of a series on the life of Muḥammad, written by Mrs Olive Toto.

## The Conversion of 'Umar

Please remember, all you little girls who will grow up to be women, that Muḥammad's first believer was a woman, Khadīja his wife . . .

His next believers were 'Alī and a little slave boy Zayd, who were about twelve or fourteen years old. Maybe they were young, but they were very serious boys and knew what they believed to be right. Abu Bakr, an old and trusted friend, joined Muḥammad. Other friends also came forward. A small band of fifty people joined Muḥammad in his belief.

Now a change came about. The citizens of Mecca turned against Muḥammad and his followers were persecuted. After three years an open opposition was organised and acts of violence started. A youth leading prayer was attacked and he fought back. Islam does not say turn the other cheek. It is common sense that one has to defend oneself.

In the fourth year of his mission, Muḥammad was given a friend's house to hold meetings for people who wanted to know about God. The name of this friend was Arqam . . .

There was a man called ʿUmar. He thought about things and decided to have his peace of mind by killing Muḥammad, and then his followers would forget him. So he took his sword in his hand and went to Muḥammad's house to kill him. ʿUmar was a man of great influence in Mecca. He did not know that his sister Fāṭima and her husband had become Muslims. On his way to the Prophet's house with his sword in his hand he met a man who had recently embraced Islam. Seeing the sword the man said, "Where are you going?" ʿUmar said, "To kill Muḥammad." "Oh," said the man, "don't you know that even your sister and your brother-in-law have embraced Muḥammad's religion?"

ʿUmar was furious: he decided his relations must die first and then Muḥammad. On reaching the house he heard his relatives reading verses that had been revealed to Muḥammad from God. ʿUmar was so furious that he beat his brother-in-law very badly. ʿUmar's sister was hurt whilst trying to stop the fight. ʿUmar snatched away these verses and started to read them. One could have heard a pin drop, so engrossed was ʿUmar. His rage had calmed down, and his breathing was once more like a human being's. Gradually, as he was reading the words, peace came into his heart. He was reading something that calmed his soul with its truth and beauty. It had set him thinking.

On seeing this altered man, the followers talked to him, and soon the harsh and proud ʿUmar joined Islam.

ʿUmar then went to the house of Arqam, where Muḥammad met him at the door. ʿUmar said, "O Prophet of God! I declare my faith in God and believe in His Prophet." Things became much easier with ʿUmar on Muḥammad's side.

## Mary and Jesus

Of all the women honoured in the Qur'ān, Mary mother of Jesus stands highest. Her own family upbringing is recounted in the third sūra of the Qur'ān, which is named after her father 'Imrān. The visit of the angel, and the birth of Jesus, are told more than once. Here is the story as it is given in the chapter named after Mary:

In the name of God, the Merciful, the Compassionate.
And make mention of Mary in the Scripture, when she had withdrawn from her people to a chamber looking East,
And had chosen seclusion from them. Then We sent unto her
Our spirit and it assumed for her the likeness of a perfect man.
She said: Lo! I seek refuge in the Beneficent One from thee, if thou art God-fearing.
He said: I am only a messenger of thy Lord, that I may bestow on thee a faultless son.
She said: How can I have a son when no mortal hath touched me, neither have I been unchaste?
He said: So (it will be). Thy Lord saith: It is easy for Me. and (it will be) that We may make of him a revelation for mankind and a mercy from Us, and it is a thing ordained.

And she conceived him, and she withdrew with him to a far place.
And the pangs of childbirth drove her unto the trunk of the palm tree.
She said: Oh, would that I had died ere this, and had become a thing of naught, forgotten!
Then (one) cried unto her from below her, saying: Grieve not!
Thy Lord hath placed a rivulet beneath thee,
And shake the trunk of the palm tree toward thee, thou wilt cause ripe dates to fall upon thee.
So eat and drink and be consoled. And if thou meetest any mortal, say: Lo! I have vowed a fast unto the Beneficent, and may not speak this day to any mortal.

Then she brought him to her own folk, carrying him.
They said: O Mary! Thou hast come with an amazing thing.
Oh sister of Aaron! Thy father was not a wicked man nor was thy mother a harlot.
Then she pointed to him. They said: How can we talk to one who is in the cradle, a young boy?

He spake: Lo! I am the slave of Allah. He hath given me the Scripture and hath appointed me a Prophet,

And hath made me blessed wheresoever I may be, and hath enjoined upon me prayer and almsgiving so long as I remain alive,
And (hath made me) dutiful toward her who bore me, and hath not made me arrogant, unblest.
Peace be upon me the day I was born, and the day I die, and the day I shall be raised alive!

Such was Jesus, son of Mary.

Qur'ān: Sūra 19: 16–34 Mary

"The beginning of wisdom is the fear of God"

London Central Mosque, 1976

# PART THREE
## *Bridges*

# CHAPTER EIGHT

# *The Bridge from Man to Man*

If any show patience and forgive, that truly would be an exercise of courageous will and resolution in the conduct of affairs.

Qur'ān: Sūra 42: 43 *Counsel*

A good Muslim is a forgiver.

Dr 'Abd al-Rahmān 'Azzām

Reciprocity is the legal rule. Forgiveness is the moral principle. As long as you limit yourself to reciprocity, you are on the human level. You go beyond it to forgiveness, and you reach the higher, divine level.

Dr Hassan Saab[1]

In bridging the gap between man and man forgiveness plays an essential part. Magnanimity is a sign of strength.

What is recommended is not a "mercy out of weakness", such as Muslims feel the Sermon on the Mount advocates. It is a "mercy out of power". An example of this is Muḥammad's grant of an amnesty to the Meccans when he re-entered their city. Muhammad Husayn Haykal, modern biographer of the Prophet, says, "Muḥammad was not a tyrant or a proud person. God had given him power over his enemies and while he had the power he forgave."[2]

There is much to be learned from the Qur'ān on the subject of forgiveness, and the application of its teachings raises many questions for those who seek to follow its injunctions.

Ceiling design
Bursa, Turkey, 1421 AD

# Forgiveness in the Qur'ān

In the Muslim view, there are two sides to the question of forgiveness: God's relationship to man, and man's relationship to his fellow men.

God is full of forgiveness, the great Forgiver. He is "ample in forgiveness." (Sūra 53: 32 *The Star*) Man can and must ask forgiveness for his sins. David did so in repentance, and received forgiveness. (Sūra 38: 25–26 *Ṣād*.)

The commentaries on the Qur'ān all give notes on the verses relating to the receiving of forgiveness, and the injunctions to forgive. In *The Holy Qur'ān – Text, Translation and Commentary*, by Abdullah Yusuf Ali, there is a note on the words used in the Qur'ān for forgiveness. These are three. One (*'afā*) means to forget, to obliterate from one's mind. Another (*sāmaḥa*) means to overlook, to turn away from, ignore, treat a matter as if it did not affect one. The most common (*ghafara*) means to cover up something, as God does to our sins with His grace. "This word is particularly appropriate in God's attribute of *Ghaffār*, One who forgives again and again."[3]

The one unforgivable sin is to put anyone or anything in the place God alone should hold, to associate anything else with Him. "God forgiveth not that partners should be set up with Him: but He forgiveth anything else, to whom He pleaseth." (Sūra 4: 48 *Women*) Yusuf Ali comments that this is because such an association is what treason would be in an earthly kingdom. It is "rebellion against the essence and source of spiritual life."

Believers are told, "Be foremost in seeking forgiveness" (Sūra 57: 21 *Iron*); "Race towards forgiveness from your Lord" (Sūra 3: 133 *Imrān*); and in the next verse "Restrain anger and pardon men." (Sūra 3: 134 *Imrān*)

"Forgive, even when angry," is one of the duties of believers, given in the Sūra of Counsel (Sūra 42: 37 *Counsel*). These duties also include resisting wrongful oppression. The text continues, "Let evil be rewarded with evil. But he that forgives and seeks reconcilement shall be rewarded by God. He does not love wrongdoers." (Sūra 42: 40 *Counsel*)

"If we tolerate wrong," comments Yusuf Ali, "by allowing it to run rampant when we can prevent it, we fail in our duty to God." The same thought is in the verse, "Fight for the cause of God against those who fight against you: but do not attack, for God does not love the aggressors." (Sūra 2: 190 *The Cow*)

The way to meet evil, however, is by good. "Repel evil with what is better." (Sūra 23: 96 *Believers*, Sūra 13: 22 *Thunder*)

"Let them forgive and overlook. Do you not wish that God should forgive you?" (Sūra 24: 22 *Light*) An attitude of forgiveness is necessary in dealing with opposition. As for those who oppose the message through "selfish envy", "Forgive and overlook, till God accomplish His purpose." (Sūra 2: 109 *The Cow*) "Tell those who believe to forgive those who do not look forward to the days of God. It is for Him to recompense (for good or ill) each People, according to what they have earned." (Sūra 45: 14–15 *Crouching*) Yusuf Ali's comment: it is not for private persons to take vengeance, they should leave it to God.

"Requite evil with good, and he who is your enemy will become your dearest friend." (Sūra 41: 34 *Expounded*) Forgiveness can bring about a change in the situation. Yusuf Ali comments on the duty of forgiveness:

> It is harder to be patient and forgive, and yet to get wrongs righted, as was done by the Holy Prophet, than to bluster about and "punish the guilty" or "teach them lessons". It may look like futility and lack of purpose. but in reality it is the highest and noblest form of courage and resolution. And it may carry out the purpose of reform and the suppression of evil even better than stern punishment . . . In some cases severity may be called for, but it must be from a strict judicial motive and not merely from personal anger or spite or any lower motive in disguise.[4]

Yusuf Ali comments also on the teaching in the Old and New Testaments in relation to retaliation. The Qur'ān says: "We (God) revealed to Moses the Law . . . We ordained therein for them life for life, eye for eye, nose for nose, ear for ear, tooth for tooth, and wounds equal for equal. But if anyone remits the retaliation by way of charity, it is an act of atonement for himself." (Sūra 5: 45 *The Table*) The comment:

> The retaliation is prescribed in three places in the Pentateuch . . . In none of them is found the additional rider for mercy, as here. Note that in *Matthew* 5:38 Jesus quotes the old Law, "eye for eye" etc., and modifies it in the direction of forgiveness, but the Qur'ānic injunction is more practical.[5]

# Forgiveness from Strength

Forgiveness is a virtue of the strong. "Justice is tightly bound to mercy. When Islam places justice next to mercy, it places forgiveness next to justice – on condition that it is forgiveness while one is strong."

In conversation, Dr Ali Issa Othman, Palestinian sociologist, clarified this:

Question:     What is Islam's teaching on forgiveness?

Dr Othman:     Forgiveness is an old Arab tradition. Islam did not introduce something entirely new. One of the signs of power is to forgive. It is part of being manly, you are bigger and more powerful if you forgive. There is a much prized quality, *ḥilm*, magnanimity: not easily excited to wrath. A man, in order to be counted as a man, must have such traits of character.

Question:     You see forgiveness as a sign of power?

Dr Othman:     Yes. If you forgive when you are weak, no one will ever know if it is weakness you show, or forgiveness. It *may* be the latter, genuine forgiveness. But how do we know? If it is known that you are in a position *not* to forgive, and then you do forgive, then that is a very highly considered trait.

This was so before Islam, and was carried on in Islam. Most of the great Islamic values in human contacts were already there before the Prophet came. The words for them were already in the Arabic language. Monotheism gathered them all up, and utilised them for a higher purpose.

For an Arab to strike the weaker always reflects on him very badly. If your adversary is strong, it is a matter of pride to fight him. For instance, the annals on the Crusades delight to show how strong the Crusaders were: it was a credit to us therefore to fight them well. But if your adversary is weak, it is not so creditable to fight him. We would rather forgive. Take Israel. Our tradition tells us that they are a weak people. But Israel has manifested that they are stronger than we are. Therefore there is an internal conflict. Should we forgive them? Or should we fight them well, because we discover they are very strong?

Question:     What about forgiveness in human relationships?

Dr Othman:     If so and so is a strong man, with many men around him, and something is done against him by some weak man with few men, he will not react in the same way as he would towards a strong man. He would rather forgive. It is expected of him. It is a sign of his strength. This is the ideal, and it is found on all levels.

In the Qur'ān, what is emphasised about such reaction is self-defence. "If they attack you, attack them in like manner as they attacked you." (Sūra 2: 194 *The Cow*) In another verse, it is said that it is better that you forgive. You are capable of doing so. The idea of the ability to forgive is always there. Then your enemy may become your closest friend, through forgiveness.

Question:    You always envisage this from a position of strength?

Dr Othman:   It is so in tradition, yes.

Question:    Is this a limitation?

Dr Othman:   No. Forgiveness by the weak may be genuine, but we can never know, and that is why forgiveness by the strong is emphasised. But forgiveness by the weak is not excluded, and in later thought in Islam such acts of forgiveness became acts which in themselves purified the self. If I forgive you, I do not just help you. By the same act I am making myself better. This is the idea behind the word *Tazkiyeh*, purifying the self from human reactions.[6]

Tile: "In very truth, there is no God but Allah"
Turkey, 17th century AD

# The Delhi Carpenters

The way in which the truths of forgiveness and give-and-take are related to the lives of ordinary people may be illustrated by a conversation with a group of Indians, carpenters from near Delhi.

For centuries, since the construction of the glorious buildings of the Mogul period, the carpenters of Delhi have maintained a tradition of skill in carving and woodwork. In 1971, a group of craftsmen came to work on the construction of a large centre at Panchgani, Maharashtra.[7] When they arrived one morning after three days of travel, they were offered the day off. "Please take us to the timber," said their leader, Bunyad Khan. "Our hearts want to work." Later they kept the fast of Ramaḍān, working through the days, without food or drink from dawn till sunset, and included everyone on the site in celebrating the breaking of the fast. Hindu and Christian, Indian and European, all learned much from their skill and dedication. Now they were about to take a holiday, and go home for the next great feast, the "Īd al-Aḍḥā, the Feast of Sacrifice, the climax of the month of pilgrimage.

On the morning before their journey, they invited me to visit them, with an interpreter, a young Hindu journalist for whom the exploration of the truths of Islam was new ground. We sat outside their quarters, and talked of their homes and of the feast which was about to take place.

They expressed their joy that they would be back in their villages and described exactly what they would do. On the tenth day of the month, all the men would dress in their best and go to the Idgah, an open place of worship. Here they would give praise to God and thank Him for the opportunity of life and for His provision. They would also ask His forgiveness for their past sins.

A lively discussion then took place on the question of forgiveness, including the search for the right word in Urdu to convey the idea. In an article the following week, the Hindu journalist wrote:

> "What should we do when someone has hurt us?" someone asked. A warm discussion ensued. Mohammed Ishaq (one of the carpenters) explained, capturing the mike over a babble of voices, that there were two aspects to this question. One was related to man's right on man, the other to God's right on man. "If I have hurt another," he said, "I must ask for his forgiveness and try my best to make him happy. I will never be able to make him happy just by giving him clothes, money or material possessions, as I would by making an apology to him."

We moved on to the subject of forgiveness. Bunyad Khan, who had so far been silent, said in his quiet voice, "If I have made a mistake and I repent, promising not to repeat the mistake, then Allah forgives." He quickly added, "However there is one sin that Allah does not forgive. If I put something else, be it man or money, in God's place, God does not forgive that." He added, a little later, with all the wisdom of his years, "Life is a fight between good and evil, and that is the greatest *Jihād* (struggle) in the human heart."[8]

One of the carpenters is a *ḥāfiz*: one who knows the whole Qur'ān by heart. As our discussion ended with an invitation to visit their families and villages, his beautiful voice rang out over the hillside. Then silence fell. Later in the day, before leaving, one of the men himself set right a dispute which had taken place some days previously. "I must not covet, and envy the rich," he said. "I must treat rich and poor alike. To confront and battle with desires, and to keep my heart satisfied – that is also the greatest *Jihād*."

Tomb of Akbar: gateway
Sikandra, India

# Turning Enemies into Friends

The late Dr Abderrahman al-Bazzaz, ambassador and scholar, was the first Secretary General of OPEC, and for a few months in 1967 Prime Minister of Iraq. In these positions he undertook many difficult negotiations. Asked "What is the inspiration behind your handling of affairs of state?", he replied:

I am a believer in Islam, and its spiritual and dogmatic principles. Islam means to yield to the Will of God, and to believe in the unity of mankind.

Forgiveness is constant in the Qur'ān. God is the Forgiver. "Forgiveness is the nearest to piety (taqwā)." There is God's forgiveness to men – and there is forgiveness between individuals. This can also apply between nations. Enemies can be turned into friends.

The Fātiḥa (opening chapter of the Qur'ān) is a reminder to every leader and responsible man. Every Muslim reads the Fātiḥa, at the beginning of every prayer. There is much thought and meaning in it. First, you pray to God Who is merciful and compassionate. The next phrase is Lord of the *world* – not just the Arabs or the Muslims but the whole world.

Then comes, "Owner of the Day of Judgment". This is a reminder – to every statesman, every responsible person, every individual – of the fact that he will be held responsible for what he does. It means that God knows what you try to hide.

This consciousness of God's knowledge of events has a great effect. It gives a man courage and self control, in his actions, in his words and even in his thinking. It gives him a guidance from within and has a great influence on his behaviour as a man and as a ruler.

"We pray to You, and to You alone." The translation of this is not always clear. 'Iyyāka means "You alone". It means that there is no worship, no service, but of God. There is no help or respect from any other source, and no superiority. Only God will judge a man. All his actions, and his feelings and emotions, must be directed to Him alone.

This reminds every ruler and responsible man to be careful. He must be cautious, judicious, courageous. All his feelings must be directed to one purpose: for the sake of God. And I mean something realistic by this: the service of the people of God.[9]

# "It is Good to Forgive, Better to Forget"

The Maqassed Islamiyyah Association, Beirut, is among the large private educational organisations in the Muslim world. Founded in 1877, it financed schools in Beirut and in the villages of Lebanon. In the early 1970s, twenty-five thousand boys and girls were attending these.

Its secondary school for girls, named after the general Khālid ibn al-Walīd, drew pupils from many parts of the Arab World. Miss Ihsan Mahmassani, as its Principal, built up the school from four hundred to over fourteen hundred. She is proud of the growth in scientific studies now available for women, and of the doctors and scientists among her old pupils. But, she says, the most important thing for the girls is that they should be able to train their own children. The level of education is rising and will continue to do so, as educated parents bring up their children. At the same time the level of character is not necessarily rising. Pressures from the West do not help this. It is vital that the traditional teaching of the Qur'ān and religion is made relevant to the needs of modern life.

One of her staff, Miss Hassiba Ghorayib, showed me a set of compositions written by girls of twelve years old, illustrating the type of character training given.[10] "I often set them subjects that are going round in my own mind," she said. This one was on the question of forgiveness: "It is good to forgive, better to forget."

> Everyone in this world makes mistakes. He loves, hates, does different wrong things, sometimes against the law such as killing and stealing.
>
> Sometimes a person does something wrong to his friend and then he apologises. If his friend really wants to forgive him, he will forget what he has done to him. But if not he will forgive him only, and every time he will remind him, and they will not be friends any more.
>
> So everyone must forgive the one who is mistaken and forget his mistake because sometimes he may do mistakes (himself) and need someone to forgive him.
>
> Once my friend made me angry and on the second day she came and said: "Good morning." So I supposed she wanted me to talk to her and not to be angry with her any more. I forgave her but I did not forget the incident at all. If a person remembers the faults of his enemy towards him, he will hate all other people, because everyone in this world makes mistakes. We should not have bad feeling against people, because men have to share other people's life.

Life is a hard way, and everyone makes mistakes except God. If a person was doing good to us, then does something wrong and hurts us, we should not forget his kindness before.

There is something that God has put in every human being. This thing is called conscience. It guides everyone to do good deeds, and warns everyone against doing bad. The one who has a good conscience is able to forgive others.

If a person helps us, he must not every time say that he helped us. He must forget and help us.

It is better if we forgive each other than to keep ourselves sad. It is better to forget the incident than to hold a grudge. If two friends quarrel they must forget every bad thing they did to each other, to be good citizens for our country.

If a youth spends his money, and speaks in a bad way with his father and mother, at first they punish him but afterwards they forget what he has done wrong. When this person sees that his father treats him well after what he has done, he becomes ashamed of himself and becomes a good boy. So we notice that forgiving has its effect on the character of the person who has been forgiven.

It is better to forgive and forget at the same time, so that we will be human in the true sense of the word.

# Assassin and Victim: Who Wins?

"God forgives, and so must we," said a Turkish editor when asked about the place of forgiveness in Islamic teaching.

Dr Ahmet Emin Yalman, founder and for twenty years editor of the Turkish daily *Vatan* (Fatherland), was born in Salonika in 1888. On many occasions he played a reconciling role in his own country, as he also did at a time of acute tension between Turkey and Greece over Cyprus in 1958. "He laid aside old prejudices, went to Athens and wrote a statesmanlike article which was given front-page coverage in the Greek press," said a Greek correspondent. *The Times* of London wrote (8 March 1960), "Probably no Turk has achieved more respect among all communities during the recent years in Cyprus than Mr Yalman. His moderate and conciliatory writings on the Cyprus question and Graeco-Turkish relations are considered to have helped create the atmosphere which made the Zürich agreement possible."

In December 1972, he died in Istanbul, aged eighty-four. Many tributes were paid to his role in the birth and struggles of the new Turkey. One of these was by a lawyer, Hüseyin Üzmez. As a young, idealistic student twenty years before, Üzmez had been in a plot to kill Yalman. When he heard of Yalman's death, he told his own story of the attempted assassination and its sequel. "How many of us," he said, "are able to conquer even the hearts of our enemies as did Ahmet Emin Yalman?"

In 1952, Yalman was in the city of Malatya, at the same time as Prime Minister Menderes. Malatya was a stronghold of the opposition party, but at a dinner given for the Prime Minister speeches were made on both sides stressing the need for unity in accomplishing national goals.

Shortly before midnight, Yalman left the table to telephone the story to his paper. As he left the door, a hail of bullets hit him.

The would-be assassin was a high-school student. He was sentenced to twenty years' imprisonment. Yalman kept in touch with him, and arranged for him to continue his legal studies in prison. "What a sad coincidence that the very day I opened my own lawyer's office in Ankara, the radio announced his death," says that student, Hüseyin Üzmez, in an article published on 31 December 1972, in the liberal daily, *Milliyet*.

## I Tried to Kill Yalman

I first met him exactly twenty years ago when I was an eighteen-year-old school student. I sincerely believed that Ahmet Emin Yalman should be assassinated. He had arrived in Malatya with Prime Minister Adnan Menderes and, shortly before midnight, I managed to get close to him and fired six shots.

He was taken to hospital in a coma. He regained consciousness two days later and asked to see me, whereupon I was taken to his bedside. He was in bandages and had difficulty in speaking. I introduced myself to him as "your enemy" though there he no longer seemed like one. He said how he pitied my mother, working very hard in a factory to provide me with a good education and future. "Thank God that I have survived," he told me, "but how I regret the years of your youth which will go to waste." Despite myself, his words impressed me and there were tears in my eyes. But I could not believe him; I refused to believe him; I was still fired with excitement though inexperienced and not yet hardened by life.

Then came investigations, courts, and the sentence to twenty years in prison. I was handcuffed and taken from town to town, prison to prison.

Still I was not sorry. I would not believe, even to myself, that I had done anything wrong.

Years passed, conditions changed and coups d'état were followed by Government changes.

After the 27 May revolution (1960),[11] the press was enjoying a freedom till then unknown.

The journalists became the "wise men" of the country, their advice being sought on every matter. Yalman was at their head.

There were rumours in the prisons of an amnesty and even the perpetrators of these lies convinced themselves of their truth. Everyone was excited, cheerful and daydreaming. Not me; deep down I was scared. I was sure that Yalman and those under his influence would oppose the amnesty. Though my prison mates kept quiet, I was sure they felt the same.

Suddenly one morning, the door of my dormitory was flung open and a few of my friends dashed in waving a newspaper and shouting "Look what your man has written!"

The newspaper was *Vatan*, Mr Yalman's paper, and the banner headline read "Hüseyin Üzmez deserves forgiveness."

In his leading article, Ahmet Emin Yalman praised me and insisted on my release. It was a peculiar feeling. Eight years in prison had taught me a great deal about life and I was no longer inflexible. I was grateful to Mr Yalman not just for my own happiness but for my thousands of fellow prisoners. I could not bring myself, however, to express these sentiments by word or letter for fear of embarrassing myself before the enemy.

Shortly afterwards I received a letter from him asking to visit me. After much hesitation I replied, and this was the start of an active correspondence between us. He also sent me collections of his articles and as soon as I read them I realised how wrong I had been about him.

One day he came to see me. I was then in Izmir prison and we met in the governor's office. We shook hands and I said to him: "Years ago I was of the sincere belief that you should be got rid of, which is why I fired at you. Since I was genuinely sincere at the time, I do not regret what I did, but, having come to know you, I realise that it was a mistake."

He greeted me like an old friend, his eyes sparkling, and said that he wanted my release more than I wanted it myself. He was sorry, he said, about my mother, who was still working in the factory, but glad that I had not allowed myself to get too depressed. He congratulated me on my efforts to complete my education in prison and asked me how I had progressed with my English. Would I, he wondered, be able to understand the English books which he intended to send me. I replied: "If you like, we can converse in English." The rest of our conversation was in English and we talked for about two hours. Then he asked me if he could give me a present.

"If it is a book or a box of chocolates," I replied, "then I shall be grateful, but please, if it is something else, excuse me and do not be offended if I refuse. Please try to understand."

He was fighting back tears as he left.

As a result of the general amnesty in 1960, my sentence was reduced by half. After ten years and three days I was a free man again.

Outside it was not as I had imagined and I had many burdens to bear. I had no job, no money, my mother was paralysed and about to die and, in the meantime, I was attending lectures at the Law Faculty.

Mr Yalman was trying to help me without offending me. One evening a limousine pulled up in front of the shack in which I was then living and I was told, "Deputy Prime Minister Kemal Satir wishes to see you." He received me with great kindness and said that he was trying to find me a job with the local council.

I had written a book during my years in prison and Mr Yalman was insisting on its publication. Since it contained my old views, I felt it should be revised and I was not happy with it; nor, did I think, would Mr Yalman be either, though I was too proud to tell him. He insisted on reading it, however, and a few days later I received a letter from him. "I am very disappointed," he wrote. "You could be a liberal and progressionist leader. Your book is full of hatred and fanaticism."

It seemed that our ties were about to break, but in fact the contrary happened and, with the help of the late Professor Fikret Arik, he secured me a scholarship.

What a sad coincidence that the very day I opened my own lawyer's office in Ankara, the radio announced his death.

I do not mind if I am criticised by some circles; I have no fears and expect favouritism from no one. My conscience and chivalry require that I tell the truth.

How many of us are able to conquer even the hearts of our enemies as did Ahmet Emin Yalman?

Our views may have differed, but Mr Yalman as I knew him was a sensitive man, full of goodness and modesty, with ready tears in his eyes. I am jealous of his greatness.

May God's blessings be upon him.

Hüseyin Üzmez[12]

Tile: "There is no victor but God"
Alhambra, 14th century AD

# CHAPTER NINE

## *The Bridge from War to Peace*

The Prophet reckoned the battle with
oneself as the greatest struggle (*jihād*).
As he returned from one of his
expeditions he said, 'We have come
back from the lesser *jihād* to the greater
*jihād*.' He meant the struggle with
one's own passions.

Shaikh Muhammad Ahmad Surur, Asmara

If there existed between my adversary
and myself even a camel's hair I would
not cut it off: if he pulled the hair I
would loosen it: if he loosened it, I
would pull it.

The Umayyad Caliph Mu'awiya[1]

Each time that men by negotiation and
good will succeed in finding an answer
to the conflict of powerful national
interests, the whole world from East to
West should pause for a moment in
silence, meditate on the lesson and
draw from it fresh inspiration.

President Habib Bourguiba[2]

To build the bridge from war to peace is one of the constant preoccupations of human history. Muslims are deeply involved in many such negotiations today.

Their approach is realistic:

> As long as war resides in the nature of man, all that can be attained is the greatest possible limitation of it. The most that one may expect is that there will be war only in defence of the faith, and of freedom of opinion and the propagation of it. This is what Islam determined, and what is revealed in the Qur'ān.[3]

The word *Islām* is connected with peace. Peace is healthy, war is a disease, says Dr Abdel Khalek Hassouna, who as Secretary General of the Arab League was for many years at the heart of negotiations in the Arab World. Peace-making is an honourable art, with a long history starting with the Prophet himself. Instances of this are given in this chapter.

At the same time, Islam calls for struggle, *jihād*, in the path of God. The nature of this struggle is also examined.

"Wars, wars, wars," said an international jurist, Dr Sobhi Mahmassani. "What else is there in the history books? Islam has tried to regulate them, as has every other system."

A twice-repeated prayer: "O Victor!"

# Peace-Making: An Honourable Art

To the Muslim, peace-making is an honourable art, a duty, and one for which the Prophet himself was noted. He waged war when he felt driven to it by his enemies. He also reconciled the warring tribes of Arabia.

Two events are illuminating in this connection. One is the victorious entry of Muḥammad into Mecca. The second is the treaty made by the Caliph 'Umar with the inhabitants of Jerusalem after its conquest a few years later.

Muḥammad left his native city of Mecca in AD 622 rejected and persecuted. Eight years later he re-entered it as a conqueror, with his persecutors in his power. That moment is often described as his greatest victory – the victory being over himself. Dr Muhammad Hoballah, late Imam of the Islamic Cultural Centre, London, addressing a gathering of several hundred in honour of the Prophet's Birthday (6 April 1974), referred to the amnesty given to the Meccans. In that captured city, he said, no house was robbed, no woman insulted, only the idols were destroyed. An Arab Prime Minister, Dr Abderrahman al-Bazzaz, said:

> Muḥammad's work was remarkable. See the way he turned enemies into friends by forgiveness. For instance, when he conquered Mecca, the Meccan nobles were made prisoner. They were brought before him – after all the bitterness and persecution they had inflicted on him. He asked, "What am I to do with you?" Their leader Abu Sufyan was a clever man. He said, "The best." Muḥammad said, "You are all free."[4]

Jerusalem surrendered to the Muslim armies in the year AD 638. The Caliph 'Umar himself came to take over the city, and arranged the terms. These were a model for later treaties:

> In the name of Allah, the Merciful, the Compassionate. This is the covenant which 'Umar ibn al-Khattab, the servant of Allah, the Commander of the Faithful, grants to the people of Aelia (Bait al-Maqdis). He grants them security of their lives, their possessions, their churches, their crosses ... They shall have freedom of religion and none shall be molested unless they rise up in a body. They shall pay a tax instead of military service ... and those who leave the city shall be safeguarded until they reach their destination.[5]

# The Spread of Islam

Asked about the means by which Islam was spread, Dr Ali Issa Othman replied:

The spread of Islam was military. There is a tendency to apologise for this and we should not. It is one of the injunctions of the Qur'ān that you must fight for the spreading of Islam. After the fighting was over – not just in theory but historically – the conquered people were not vanquished in the usual sense of the word. They became equal with the conquerors, if they accepted the idea of Islam, or if they were already "People of the Book" like the Christians and the Jews, who were not supposed to become Muslims. For several centuries the conquered Christians remained Christians. Then for one reason or another – whether convenience or not – most of them gradually became Muslims. But they were not compelled to do so.

Fighting for God (jihād) has a wider meaning in Islam. It may be militant, or it may be evangelical, in the Christian sense. The militant is not excluded. This is because, according to the Qur'ān, communities have always resisted a prophet's offer of guidance from God. In each case tradition was much stronger than an open mind to a new idea. So you find resistance – the traditional answer being: "We found our fathers worshipping in this way, and we shall continue."

Jihād may be a matter of persuasion. It may also be a preparation, producing conditions in which people will be receptive. Historically, military means were used to do this. It was part of being an early Muslim, to join in the military arrangements of the Muslims. Why you fight is important. It is quite clear that they did not go out to acquire wealth, land, riches, though these were a by-product. Their purpose was to fight in the path of God.

Why is it that we in this part of the world are now so staunchly proud to be Arabs and Muslims, when originally we were not from Arabia and were conquered people? In other empires people were never willing to identify themselves with their conquerors. They rebelled. This is the key to the whole question. The treatment was different, and the relationship. The Arab did not fight in order to become master. He fought for a certain set of principles. Whether you approve or not of what he did is another matter, but you can try to understand it.

Dr Ali Issa Othman[6]

# War, Pollution and the "Greater Jihād"

Islam enjoins fighting a holy war (*jihād*), as well as promising peace. In a modern setting, what is this "war" fought for? And what is it fought against?

In answer to this question, the following observations were made by Professor Yusuf Ibish, Professor of Islamic Political Theory and Institutions, American University of Beirut. He clarifies the dual nature of *Jihād*, and links it today with the crucial question of man's dealing with his environment:

> The question of *Jihād* (Holy War) has been misunderstood. It is essentially divided into two.
>
> The Greater *Jihād* is fighting one's animal tendencies. It is internal rather than external: striving in the path of God to overcome one's animal side. Man shares with animals certain characteristics which, if let loose, make him a very dangerous beast. To bring those passions under control, that is what *Jihād* means. Man has a tendency to overestimate himself – and to underestimate his spiritual potential. He has a tendency to control and exploit his environment, and other human beings. *Jihād* is essentially against such tendencies.
>
> The Lesser *Jihād* – fighting on behalf of the community, in its defence – is a duty incumbent on a Muslim provided he is attacked. A man has the right to defend his life, his property, and he has to organise himself along these lines.
>
> Of course one can produce incidents in history, and ask whether in fact the principle of self-defence applies. It is true that Muslims have waged wars: wars of conquest, wars in the ordinary sense, often not at all related to religion or faith. But this indicates that some Muslims have not exercised the Greater *Jihād*.
>
> The whole issue is coloured in the western mind by the historical encounters which have taken place. I am well aware of the fact that the Muslims broke out into the world aggressively, and challenged the Christian world on its own ground, both militarily and theologically; and brought large portions of Europe under their domain. The "carte de visite" was returned by the Crusaders, and in the name of Christianity – of the Cross – all sorts of horrors were committed. Then the Muslims, led by the Ottoman Turks, returned the "carte de visite" once more, knocking at the gates of Vienna and conquering the Balkans. There was another encounter in the Nineteenth Century, when Egypt was occupied in the Napoleonic wars, followed by Algeria. Gradually great

areas of Muslim lands were brought under western control, from Morocco to Indonesia. All this of course involved a great deal of organised fighting in defence of the community.

What we are facing now is a different type of aggression. Western man is trying to westernise the world, and by doing so to change the identity of those who are westernised. It is perhaps one of the most aggressive invasions of history. When the Muslims took over land populated by Christians, we have ample evidence that there were no large scale attempts to convert people by the sword, though of course there are exceptions to the rule. Essentially a Christian or a Jew could live in a Muslim-occupied territory, and practise his religion. He had to pay a certain tax, but there was no need to change his identity. In modern times, this is less and less possible. Western man is aggressively westernising, in a way that alienates a man from his true identity.

This type of aggressiveness goes with a tremendous disrespect for nature – a lack of awe and wonder at its mysteries. We exploit nature, and spoil it. We cease even to be poetic about it. The forest is so many tons of pulp and paper, rather than the handiwork of God, lovely shady trees. The landscape is simply what lies beneath it. The air is polluted, the rivers are no longer the habitat of living creatures, and a dislocation of the human soul takes place. It is not too much to say that the measure of modern man's civilisation is the amount of garbage he produces, and the amount he litters his environment.

Modern humanism is essentially man worshipping himself, putting himself back on the pedestal. He is the centre of everything, and of the universe. So he thinks he carries his own scales within himself, that he is the measure and no one else. He refuses to be bound by anything, and is proceeding to destroy himself.

When you cease to believe in God as Creator, then man becomes creator: and as God created us in His own image, we like to create others in our own image. Development has become an obsession, not only with the industrialised world but with the nations who look for industrialisation. Never in the history of mankind has man been more dangerous to himself, because of this lack of proportion between technical know-how and spiritual strength.

To fight and control these dangerous tendencies, and to cultivate the spiritual potential in each one of us, is the true and "Greater *Jihād*".[7]

# Aspects of Jihād

The word *Jihād* and the verb that goes with it mean "to strive", "to exert", to overstrain oneself. It is used often in the Qur'ān, and has been applied to many forms of action by believers. It calls for militancy in a battle between good and evil in which all must join, in the inner striving for character and in other ways. If Saladin's wars against the Crusaders were a *Jihād*, so also are the efforts to banish ignorance and poverty from villages. "Those who believe, and suffer exile and strive with might and main in God's cause, with their goods and their persons, have the highest rank in the sight of God." (Qur'ān: Sūra 9: 20 *Repentance*). The commentator Yusuf Ali, in a note on this verse, says:

> Here is a good description of *Jihād*. It *may* require fighting in God's cause, as a form of self-sacrifice. But its essence consists in: (1) a true and sincere faith which so fixes its gaze on God, that all selfish and worldly motives seem paltry and fade away; and (2) an earnest and ceaseless activity, involving the sacrifice (if need be) of life, person or property, in the service of God. Mere brutal fighting is opposed to the whole spirit of *Jihād*, while the sincere scholar's pen or the preacher's voice or the wealthy man's contributions may be the most valuable form of *Jihād*.[8]

## "Are There Locks on Their Minds?"

The service of the mind can be as much a form of "striving" as any other. An example is the work of Maulana Abul Kalam Azad. A close colleague of Gandhi in the Indian Independence movement, he carried forward the revival of Islam already initiated by such men as the philosopher Muhammed Iqbal, and Syed Ahmad Khan, founder of the Muslim University, Aligarh.

Azad was born in 1888 in Mecca. His father was in exile there, following the uprising against the British in 1857. He gave his son a traditional education and it was not till after his death that Azad was able to venture into modern studies. In his twenties he was already a national figure, as a scholar and poet. He set aside his literary work to take on with Gandhi and others the struggle for national freedom, but he never ceased to pursue the interpretation of the Qur'ān. His aim was that its truths might come to his people in their original freshness. The result was his book, *Tarjumān al-Qur'ān*, an Urdu interpretation and commentary later produced in English. Its language is simple and direct. He himself says that he tested what he wrote on a boy of fifteen, to make sure it was clear. He tries to show what type of mind the Qur'ān seeks to build, and to break away from mechanical repetition: "Do they meditate on the Qur'ān – or are there locks on their minds?" he quotes. (Qur'ān: Sūra 47: 24 *Muḥammad*).

The work was done in and out of prison. Begun in 1915, the manuscript was twice destroyed when he was arrested. It was finally re-written in Meerut Jail in 1930, and the second edition was revised in Ahmednagar prison in 1945. But it is not the struggle against Britain for independence which is referred to as his *jihād*. It is his own development of an independent mind and a modern outlook – modern not in the sense of doing away with the old, but of clearing away what might obscure the truth. "He had to break with unthinking allegiance to mere tradition," says the foreword to the *Tarjumān*. "This struggle in its deeper reaches was at first a struggle against his own self, his very upbringing, a veritable *jihād* so to say against his own personality as built up by mediaevalism in religion to which he was heir." He had to free his mind from the clutches of his past and seek fresh avenues of approach to the sources of his faith. Writing in 1945, thirty years after he began his book, he thus describes his own struggle:

What my family traditions, education and social environment had offered me in the making of my mind I was from the very beginning of my life reluctant to rest content with ... There is hardly a single conviction which has not faced the test of denial. Whatever I could gather in this lengthy period of my life, in my search for Qur'ānic truth, I have tried to understand ... and lay out in this book ... [presenting in it] "No new tale of fiction, but a confirmation of previous scriptures, and an explanation of all things, and a guidance and a mercy to those who believe." (Qur'ān: Sūra 12: 111 *Joseph*)

Maulana Abul Kalam Azad[9]

# Bridge or Battleground

One of the best-known elder statesmen in the Arab World is Abdel Khalek Hassouna, Secretary General of the Arab League from 1952 to 1971. He was born in 1898. His grandfather held the highest religious post in Egypt, that of Shaikh al-Azhar. Abdel Khalek was sent not to Al-Azhar but to the universities of Cairo and Cambridge. He pursued a distinguished diplomatic career in the inter-war years. During World War II he held cabinet posts in Egypt, and it was from the Ministry of Foreign Affairs that he moved to the Arab League.

His varied diplomatic posts involved him in negotiations in the Middle East – that bridge or battleground in world affairs – during almost half a century of turbulent history. *The Times* once described him as "an expert in swift action in equalising disputes and finding points on which two parties agree."[10] He showed himself to be a servant of peace in an age of strife, and saw in the precepts of Islam the hope of a just solution to many conflicts and problems that confronted him. In the mind of a faithful Muslim, he says, there should be a consistent motivation towards peace, however much he feels compelled to resist injustices. He himself gave an example of such a motivation in the course of the Lebanon crisis of 1958 which brought the world to the brink of a third world war.

The crisis was essentially one of relationships between the Arab states. These then numbered ten, and all were members of the Arab League as well as of the United Nations. The world pressures of the Cold War, then at its height, made their disputes a matter of universal concern and danger. Nasser's star, rocketing to new heights following the western débâcle at Suez in 1956, was polarising the militant nationalism of the Arab World – a nationalism widely, but quite erroneously, seen by many in the West as synonymous with communism. Early in 1958, the formation of the United Arab Republic joined Syria with Egypt. In July, a revolution took place in Iraq. Lebanon and Jordan felt themselves threatened by their neighbours, and at the invitation of President Chamoun and King Hussein, United States marines and British paratroops landed. Meanwhile the Russians were moving armour south to reinforce Syria. The argument moved beyond local towards world confrontation, and the attempts to solve it were transferred to New York.

The anxieties of responsible world opinion may be followed in the columns of the London *Times*. An emergency session of the General Assembly of the United Nations was summoned on 8 August, at the request of both the United States and the USSR. It was adjourned till 13 August, when Eisenhower addressed the Assembly. The editorial on that day is headed, "In the Wrong Place", and *The Times* deplores the transference of "the most urgent and baffling problem in the world" from a possible summit meeting between the great powers to the General Assembly. A week later, "intense activity continues in the lobbies, with Russia and the western countries canvassing support," and under the heading "Lost Endeavour" it is stated that "any real possibility of an agreed settlement in the Arab world" had disappeared.

Yet on the next day, 21 August, we read the headline, "Arab States find Peace Formula", "UN delegates unanimous. Private conclave. 'New Spirit' in the Middle East". "The most significant of today's developments regarding the debate on the Middle East was the private meeting this afternoon of the ten Arab member states, at which they evolved a formula intended to present a picture of Arab fraternity such as would convince the world that there was no need for future foreign intervention in the Middle East." On 22 August, *The Times* report is headed "Unanimous UN Vote for Arab Plan". "Overnight an almost magical transformation came over the scene at this headquarters, where until yesterday the General Assembly after a week's debate on the Middle East still could not see how to extricate itself from the maze." Editorial comment runs (23 August), "The past few days have been full of pleasant surprises ... The resolution is courteously phrased. There is no hint of condemnation ... Why, it may be asked, should the ten Arab states have sponsored (it)? ... It is known that the Afro-Asian bloc were discussing a more peremptory and less constructive one ... The crisis in which the Arabs have found themselves in recent weeks has inspired them to combine in order to perform an act of constructive unity." *The Times* also comments on Israel's favourable vote on the Arab resolution.

The story is well documented in United Nations sources, and in the growing literature on "preventive diplomacy". But the accounts of these tense days in Hammarskjold's office do not wholly answer *The Times'* query as to how and why the unexpected unity came to birth. "Some fast diplomatic footwork saved the day," says one account.[11] The unanimous adoption of the Arab "good neighbour" resolution, as it came to be called, brought the proceeding "to an unexpectedly triumphant close," says another.[12] The "miracle", as the Indian observer Dayal called it, relieved and delighted Hammarskjold, who called the resolution "one of the strongest ever adopted by the United Nations."[13]

The picture of the "quiet diplomacy" which sought to create the essential will for a solution can be filled in on the Arab side. The motion, co-sponsored by all the ten Arab states represented at the Assembly, was presented by the Foreign Minister of Sudan, Sayyed Mohammed Ahmed Mahgoub, who tells the story in his book *Democracy on Trial*. "We have been dealing with a dispute among members of one family, who were frank," he said. "Therefore we were able to reach a happy conclusion."[14] *The Economist* (6 September) commented, "The Arab League has a new stature, born of its success in New York."

The Secretary General of the Arab League had no official position in the Assembly. But Hassouna was in New York, and it was in his hotel that certain meetings took place crucial to the successful resolution. The Speaker of the Jordanian House of Representatives officially thanked him, along with the heads of Arab States, for "this positive step",[15] and the *Washington Post* called the resolution a "triumph for Hassouna".

The surprise revival of Arab unity, runs the *Washington Post* report (24 August), was hatched in a series of meetings in the Hotel Pierre, called by Hassouna. Some scoffed when he first called in the top diplomats of ten Arab countries – but all came. Hassouna appealed to the Arabs to go easy on each other in their speeches in the Assembly, and the Egyptian Foreign Minister Mahmoud Fawzy, who had already set a quiet tone in his opening speech, agreed. The Assembly moved on with no visible signs of Arab Unity, and it looked like an impasse. Then Mahgoub proposed to Hassouna and the ten Arab diplomats another meeting in spite of their earlier failure. They reassembled on the night of Tuesday, 19th. A drafting group was named, including Hassouna. In spite of the disapproval of Gromyko, who tried to delay the Arab plan, the agreed motion was put forward.

In an interview shortly after the General Assembly debate, Hassouna spoke with an Indian journalist, Rajmohan Gandhi. Gandhi wrote:

> Hassouna said that on the night of 9 August as he was listening to the news in his home in Egypt he had the clear compelling thought: Go to New York. He reached the UN on Wednesday 13th, ten minutes before Eisenhower was to speak. The same day he called a meeting in his hotel of all the Arab delegates. There was no agreement.
>
> From Thursday until Tuesday a tense world waited eagerly for the results of the Soviet, Norwegian and Asian proposals. No answer was brought. On Tuesday evening Hassouna again had all the Arab group

in his Pierre Hotel room. They were all together all day Wednesday. That evening they agreed on a joint resolution.

"This is an historic and momentous occasion," said Ceylon's UN Ambassador, Sir Claude Corea, supporting the resolution on behalf of the Asian-African group.

After the voting, UN delegates came over to Hassouna and said, "That was a miracle." He replied, "It was. But I had full faith that it would happen. That is why I came."

Hassouna told me: "As I returned to my room that night I could think of nothing, do nothing, but thank God."[16]

Years later, in conversation in his home (April 1973) Hassouna recalled his experience during the Lebanon crisis, as an example of God's direction in a difficult situation. An attitude of listening to thoughts that come when attuned to God in prayer – and carrying them out – can bring inspired guidance into even the most difficult affairs of modern life, he said. Had he not cultivated the habit of expecting such guidance, he would probably never have gone to New York at that time. He had just returned from an exhausting trip to Japan. Resting in bed, he pondered the news from the UN, and the thought that he was needed there ran counter to all his desires. In New York, he set to work to bridge the gulf of bitter division between the two groupings of Arab opinion behind which the great powers had ranged in hostile confrontation. It needed hours of patient persistence to make any headway. He sought to raise the discussion above the claims and counter-claims of the opposing parties, as to who was right and who was wrong in this and that particular. Painstakingly he put forward another criterion: the objective search for what was right. As he pursued this, unity began to emerge.

It may have been this habit of seeking God's direction that attracted Hassouna to Dr Buchman and Moral Re-Armament, for he several times attended their assemblies in America and in Caux, Switzerland. Indeed this movement seems to have exercised a considerable influence on the Arab statesmen at the time, for the Prime Minister of the Sudan stated, "If the West accepts the spirit of Moral Re-Armament, she would discover an immediate response from the Arab World. With that spirit the West would cure bitterness and heal hatred." The Sudanese Prime Minister was quoted in the *State Times*, Jackson, Mississippi, in an article headed, "Survival Clue? Arab Nations Display spirit of Moral Re-Armament at UN."

Dr Hassouna and his colleagues saw in the concept of Moral Re-

Armament a timely re-emphasis in world affairs on principles deeply held in Islam, and a fresh approach which they could whole-heartedly welcome. "It is a means of restoring a sense of humanity to those who occupy positions of power and who control the fate of nations," he said. "It is one of the most significant factors on the world scene."[17] In regard to the Islamic view of peace-making he stated:

The Qur'ān always opens to the hearts of the faithful the door of hope in amity with enemies. It says:

"It may be that Allah will ordain love between you and those of them with whom you are at enmity. Allah is mighty, and Allah is forgiving, merciful."

Qur'ān: Sūra 60: 7 *She that is to be examined*

God taught man to utter the word "peace" very often, indeed every time he prays, five times a day at least. He made man greet others by saying "Peace be unto you," and taught him to answer an evil deed by a good deed.

"The good deed and the evil deed are not alike. Repel the evil deed with one that is better. Then lo! he between whom and thee there was enmity (will become) as though he was a bosom friend."

Qur'ān: Sūra 41: 34 *Expounded*

"The Muslim spares other Muslims the harm of his tongue and of his hand," said the Prophet. The Muslims should hasten to accept a call for peace, even if it be a trick during war.

"And if they incline to peace, incline thou also to it, and trust in Allah. And if they would deceive thee then lo! Allah is sufficient for thee."

Qur'ān: Sūra 8: 61–2 *Spoils of War*

A Muslim's faith in these Islamic principles is a consistent motive for seeking and making peace – first within himself, then between himself and God, and then between himself and all others, be they friends or enemies, in time of peace or in time of war. Such a motivation naturally has its impact on the mind of the Muslim, and shapes his image of normal life as God meant it to be. Peace is the genuine and cherished basis of life, and war, like disease, is a hateful incident befalling men.

The theories, practice and ethics of Islam are beyond doubt the greatest force in the Islamic world in resolving differing views and paving the way for turning enmity into friendship.[18]

# CHAPTER TEN

# *The Bridge from Race to Race*

We (God) . . . have made you nations
and tribes that ye may know one
another (and be friends). The noblest
of you, in the sight of Allah, is the best
in conduct.

Qur'ān: Sūra 49: 13 *Apartments*

There is no preference for an Arab over
a non-Arab except for his piety, and
what Allah has given him of love for
human welfare and peace.

Tradition of the Prophet Muḥammad

Can Islam give any lead to the rest of the world on the question of race relations?

Many hope that it can – the historian Arnold Toynbee among them. He says, "The extinction of race consciousness as between Muslims is one of the outstanding moral achievements of Islam, and in the contemporary world there is, as it happens, a crying need for the propagation of this Islamic virtue. The forces of racial toleration, which at present seem to be fighting a losing battle in a spiritual struggle of immense importance to mankind, might still regain the upper hand if any strong influence militating against racial consciousness were now to be thrown into the scales. It is conceivable that the spirit of Islam might be the timely reinforcement which would decide this issue in favour of tolerance and peace."[1]

Islam has a good record of racial tolerance. Its mosques, and its pilgrimage gatherings, have never known any colour bar. The message of Islam rejected any racial prejudice or superiority.

Dr Abd al-Rahman Azzam, father of the Arab League, writing in the early 1940's, dealt with Islam's answer to racial bigotry. Twenty years later he was involved in a remarkable instance of change of attitude on the colour question, when Malcolm X came on pilgrimage to Mecca.


## Racial and National Strife

Dr 'Abd al-Rahmān 'Azzām served as the first Secretary-General of the Arab League from its foundation in 1945 until 1952. Before that he had a brilliant and adventurous career. In 1912 he left his medical studies in London to fight alongside the Turks in the Balkans. At the beginning of World War II he was in the Egyptian cabinet. Pressure was put on Egypt to declare war on Britain's side. Azzam stood out against this, and the declaration was not made: but he resigned, being suspect in the eyes of the British.

It was the enforced leisure that followed this resignation which gave him the opportunity to write his book, *The Eternal Message of Muḥammad*. In his mind were the terrible upheavals of world war, its causes, and where to look for a cure. He started the book, he says, as "a serious attempt to point out the Muslim answers to today's world."[2] Published first in Arabic, and later in English and many other languages, it expresses the relevance of his faith to modern issues.

His mind ranges over the questions of war and peace, of race and class: of the conditions for the growth or decadence of civilisation. On racism, he quotes traditions of the Prophet that show the attitude of Islam from the first. One of the most lovable characters in the story of Muḥammad is the black slave Bilal, whose master tried to beat the faith out of him without success, and who was later entrusted with giving the call to prayer. "Truly I am the brother of every pious man, even if he is a slave from Abyssinia; and opposed to every villain even if he is a noble Quraishi," said the Prophet.

Dr Azzam deals with racial differences under the heading, "Trusteeship over Civilisation."

## Trusteeship over Civilisation

Civilisation belongs to no one race in particular; it benefits those who are able to sustain it until such time as, through failure to shoulder its responsibilities, they relinquish it to others more worthy of marching forward with it. History amply testifies to the fact that no one people or race has had exclusive possession of civilisation or been especially endowed with unique capacities for discernment . . .

No set of distinct racial traits with which we are familiar possessed at any time in human history a monopoly over intelligence, knowledge, and originality. What is clear is that the spirit alone illuminates the obscurities of human life once the ground has been prepared for it. The bulwark of civilisation is spirit and moral character, not material-istic force. How true the Qur'ānic law is in this respect, as revealed in the words of the Almighty: "Lo! Allah changeth not the condition of a folk until they (first) change that which is in their hearts . . ." (Qur'ān: Sūra 13: 11 *Thunder*)

If we overlook certain limited differences based on climate and other circumstances in given situations, we are on safe ground when we speak of the complete equality of human spirits . . . We are justified in saying that there is no indication of differences either in physical or in spiritual traits that would make civilisation a monopoly of a segment of man-kind. Once this becomes clear, racial doctrines crumble, as does the principle of force *qua* force as a basis for civilisation.

Abd al-Rahman Azzam[3]

# Abd al-Rahman Azzam and Malcolm X

The stormy career of the Black American Muslim, Malcolm X, is told
in his autobiography: his early sufferings after the murder of his father,
his crimes, and his change of heart in prison through some "Black
Muslims"; his disillusionment, and his turning to genuine Islam.

Dr Azzam helped in the change that took place in this man's bitter
feelings about colour, during the days of the Pilgrimage, April 1964.

I knew the man from his appearances on television in New York. I
saw these when I was in New York at the United Nations. I was
impressed by his honesty and straightforwardness. There seemed to be
something in him. He was a man with a faith, but it was faith in a
man: Elijah Mohammed, the leader of the Black Muslims. It was after
he was disillusioned with Elijah Mohammed that he came to Mecca.

I knew nothing of his coming on pilgrimage. He was stopped at
Jeddah airport because he had nothing to show that he was a Muslim.
Someone in New York had said to him, "If you are in trouble, get into
touch with Dr Azzam." So he telephoned to my son, Dr Omar Azzam,
then in charge of the reconstruction work at the Ka'ba. He went straight
to the airport to fetch him.

I was very glad to see him. Money cannot buy a room in Jeddah at
a time like that when there are such crowds arriving for the Pilgrimage.
But I had been a friend of Arabia for thirty years, and I had been given
a hotel apartment. I often stayed with my son, in his house, so I gave
Malcolm X my apartment. This was perhaps surprising, for an
unknown black man to have this accommodation in the midst of such
a throng.

There was still the business of the court that judges the credentials
of pilgrims. Twice I interfered. I said, "The man says, *lā ilāha illa
Allāhu*, 'There is no god but God,' and says he is a Muslim. What
more do you want?" I think Prince Faisal sent them a message not to
make much trouble about it. He received his certificate, and was
allowed to go on to Mecca.

Islam makes no difference because of colour. It is God's business to
judge people. Malcolm X became a good Muslim, so that he no longer
judged people on colour.

The Qur'ān says, "To you is your religion, and to me mine."[4] "There
is no force in religion."[5] "Would you force them to believe?"[6] Judging
is not our business. A good Muslim is a forgiver.

Malcolm X came back later in the year. I tried to get money for him, to build a mosque in Harlem. He had quarrelled with those who already had one there. About Elijah Mohammed, I cannot judge. I hear he says he is a prophet, and in so far as he claims this he is not a Muslim. But he did help Malcom X when he was deeply involved in crime.

Then Malcolm X was killed. He was a very honest, intelligent and clever man. He had been a criminal, and had found faith in God.[7]

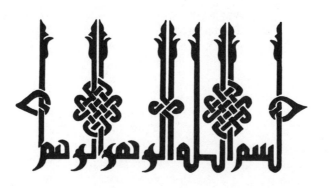

"In the Name of God, Most Gracious, Most Merciful"

# The Colour-Blindness of the Muslim World

Less than a year after his pilgrimage, Malcolm X was murdered in New York (February 1965). The final chapters of his book, written shortly before his death, give a moving account of his experiences in Mecca. Here are some extracts on his response to the hospitality of the Azzam family, and the "Colour-blindness of the Muslim world" as he found it.

First he speaks of his arrival at Jedda airport:

It was semi-dark, not long before dawn, and planes were regularly taking off and landing, their landing lights sweeping the runways, or their wing and tail lights blinking in the sky. I don't believe that motion picture cameras ever have filmed a human spectacle more colourful than my eyes took in ... Thousands upon thousands of people from all over the world made patterns of movement. I saw groups leaving for Mecca, in buses, trucks, cars. I saw some setting out to walk the forty miles ..."

There were difficulties to overcome before he could follow them. Later, as Dr Azzam's guest, he wrote:

Nothing as a black man in America had served to give me any idealistic tendencies. My instincts automatically examined the reasons, the motives, of anyone who did anything they didn't have to do for me. Always in my life if it was any white person, I could see a selfish motive.

But there in that hotel that morning ... was one of the few times I had been so awed that I was totally without resistance. That white man – at least he would have been considered "white" in America – related to Arabia's ruler, to whom he was a close advisor, truly an international man, with nothing in the world to gain, had given up his suite to me, for my transient comfort ...

That morning was the start of a radical alteration in my whole outlook about "white men".

From a letter sent to the press from Mecca:

For the past week, I have been utterly speechless and spellbound by the graciousness I see displayed all around me by people of *all colors* ... You may be shocked by these words coming from me. But on this pilgrimage, what I have seen, and experienced, has forced me to rearrange much of my thought patterns previously held, and to toss aside some of my previous conclusions ... Perhaps if White Americans could accept the Oneness of God, then perhaps, too, they could accept *in reality* the Oneness of Man – and cease to measure and hinder and harm others in terms of their "differences" in color . . . Each hour here in the Holy Land enables me to have greater spiritual insights into what is happening in America between black and white.

Shortly before his death:

I know that societies often have killed the people who have helped to change those societies. And if I can die having brought any light, having exposed any meaningful truth that will help to destroy the racist cancer that is malignant in the body of America – then, all of the credit is due to Allah. Only the mistakes have been mine.[8]

The new note of hope that Malcolm X introduced into the race struggle in America has not been without its impact. In his book *Alive to God*, Dr Kenneth Cragg refers to the conflict of motives in another Black Power leader.[9]

"In a recent book of essays,[10] Eldridge Cleaver, of the Black Panther Party in the USA, describes his uneasy turn back from total, negative hatred to a struggling sense of common humaneness, still precariously jeopardised by white arrogance, but real and precious. He ascribes his change of soul to the revolt of white youth against their 'establishment' and to the death of Malcolm X who, after pilgrimage to Mecca, repudiated the hate-philosophy of the Black Muslims in the discovery of Islam's one humanity. Cleaver writes:

'I have, so to speak, washed my hands in the blood of the martyr, Malcolm X, whose retreat from the precipice of madness created new room for others to turn about in, and I am caught up in that tiny space, attempting a manoeuvre of my own . . .' "

A review by a Muslim of Malcolm X's autobiography says:

Malcolm X (Abdul Malik Shabbaz) emerges as warm, witty and humane, and capable of tremendous drive. He is prepared only to "say like it is", and is courageous enough to change his position radically when convinced . . .

Malcolm X, though he was taken away young, has served as an inspiration for a whole generation of young negroes. On this basis he may have performed his task, but it is tempting to ponder what more he could have achieved. The emotion felt in the chapter on Ḥajj is one which any number of readings will not succeed in dimming . . . He left Mecca a new man, reaffirming for us that Islam has the only key for the realisation of a multiracial society.

When such men die, what a diminished world they leave us with.[11]

# CHAPTER ELEVEN

# The Bridge from Faith to Faith

When I understand myself, and my own beliefs, then I can understand those of others. I bow my head in reverence to God: so does the Hindu, and so does the Christian. How can I know that they do not have a more sincere faith than I do? It is in this spirit that we can co-operate together.

Mrs M. J. Haidar, for thirty two years Principal, Women's College, Aligarh Muslim University[1]

I want to be a bridge between Christianity and Islam.
There are Muslims who have betrayed the mission of Muḥammad. There are Christians who have betrayed the mission of Jesus. Let those who have not betrayed either of their missions work together.

The Rajah of Mahmudabad[2]

Much thought is given by Muslims to other religions.

Christians and Jews – "People of the Book" with their own God-given scriptures – have been for Muslims part of their world ever since the birth of Islam. In India and further East, adherents of Hinduism and the other religions of Asia are their fellow citizens.

Many examples can be given of the Muslim approach today. The answer to the question, "Do the 'People of the Book' have any common responsibility for the rest of the world?" is, "Most certainly, yes."

This common responsibility involves a co-operation of the convinced, not of the indifferent; between those who practise what they preach. As one Rector of Al-Azhar put it, "I like to meet Christians who live according to their religion."

Mosque lamp, inscribed with "The Verse of Light", Qur'ān 24: 35

14th century AD

# One Religion, Many Prophets

In 1959, the then Rector of Al-Azhar, His Eminence Shaikh Mahmoud Shaltout, gave an interview to the Canadian Ambassador in Cairo. Among the questions discussed were the following:

Question: What is the relationship between Islam and the other divine religions?

Answer: Islam does not consider that there exist religions substantially different from itself, because the religion of God is unique: it comes from one source, God Himself . . . There have been numerous prophets; each came on God's orders, to meet particular needs on earth. The Prophets took action in history. But the divine religion is one, and will remain so as God wills.

Question: What kind of relationship can there exist between those who believe in God? How can they fight effectively against materialism in all its forms, ideological, intellectual and political?

Answer: Islam affirms the unity not only of religion but of mankind. It deplores the divisions among Christians and Jews, and calls on them to be at one with the Muslims in worshipping God.

Question: How can this be made practical?

Answer: It will not be done by conferences that end as they began, in words. The only way is by enlightened thought, far-sighted culture, the road of mutual understanding. To this end each group must try dispassionately to understand deeply the principles, teachings and values of the other group. Muslims have started on this objective path. Al-Azhar has taken steps to teach foreign languages to present and former students, so that they can study foreign culture in depth, and get close to other people by understanding their ideas, values and experiences.

It is up to others to tread a similar path. Let them learn our language, study our culture and beliefs, so that they may know what we are. Thus we can meet half-way, and work together to cure the ills of humanity. Then we shall be true bearers of messages from God, believers in One God Who is Lord of all mankind.

The principle of one human family will triumph. Islam reckons this among the eternal elements in its teaching.[3]

# Al-Azhar and the Cardinal

In December 1964 the government of the United Arab Republic entertained in Cairo Cardinal Franziskus Koenig of Vienna, as he returned from the Eucharistic Congress in Bombay. He was welcomed by the officials of the University of Al-Azhar, the acknowledged intellectual centre of the Muslim world. They asked him to lecture at this venerable institution, which was then approaching its millennium and which predates the earliest of the European universities. The dialogue between Islam and Christianity has taken many forms, but it would be hard to find a parallel to this request. Not far off, Saint Francis once held discourse with the Sultan – but not exactly by invitation.

The subject chosen was "Monotheism in the Modern World". The lecture was delivered on 31 March 1965.

The Cardinal's scarlet cloak contrasted sharply with the white turbans and black cassocks of Al-Azhar's learned men. I watched and marvelled as two streams of history mingled. His Eminence the Rector of Al-Azhar University, Shaikh Ahmad Hassan al-Baqoury, together with His Eminence the Shaikh al-Azhar, highest religious authority in Islam, greeted His Eminence the Cardinal and together with the heads of faculties led him into the crowded hall. The auditorium is named after Shaikh Muhammad Abduh. That great reformer, liberaliser though he was, would have been astonished at the scene. Officially the hall holds two thousand, but the papers next morning quoted a far larger figure. Teacher and pupil from right across the Muslim world were there: students of the university and of the schools associated with it, young intellectuals who will lead the Muslim world in the next generation. With them were the leading lights of Cairo, Copt and Catholic as well as Muslim.

The Cardinal spoke of the common basis of monotheism, and the special community between Christians and Muslims which springs from their both being "People of the Book". The possibility of a mutual confrontation of common problems depends, he said, on the respect due to the other religion as a way to man's goal made possible by God, and to the principle held by Christians and Muslims alike, in spite of many misunderstandings in the course of history: "No one may be forced to believe."[4]

Prolonged applause followed his lecture. The Shaikh al-Azhar, H. E. Hassan Ma'moun, confirmed the abundant possibilities of collaboration between Muslims and Christians, as both religions face the same challenges and the same difficulties. He quoted from the Qur'ān:

"You will find the nearest in affection to those who believe are those who say, 'We are Christians.' That is because there are among them priests and monks, and because they are not proud."[5]

The dialogue continued. Shaikh Baqoury was invited to lecture in Vienna. Under the heading, "News of the Muslim World", the Al-Azhar Journal (*Majallat al-Azhar*, April 1965) noted the setting up by the Vatican of a section for Islamic Affairs. An international lawyer, Dr Sobhi Mahmassani, writing of "Islam's contribution to the human-isation of international relations", quoted the Qur'ān's command to nations "to invite to goodness, and enjoin the right and forbid the wrong" and added:

On this and other basic injunctions, which form the seed of real human civilisation, Muslims today may join hands with His Eminence Cardinal Koenig, in his remarkable appeal concluding his address at Al-Azhar University in the following terms:

"Christianity and Islam can encounter each other in a new way, one leading to a solidarity which, in this critical hour in human history, all should seek who are aware of the direction of all things towards God."

Precisely such trend is the right path for true Believers of all religions. Bitterness, hatred and rivalry among them must give place not only to negative toleration, but also to positive and fruitful co-operation on the largest possible scale.

Dr Sobhi Mahmassani, Beirut[6]

# The Muslim Approach: Some Examples

Judaism lays stress on Justice and Right: Christianity, on Love and Charity: Islam, on Brotherhood and Peace. But in the main, the fundamental similarities between the three faiths must not be lost sight of in a meticulous examination of details.

Asaf A. A. Fyzee[7]

The Holy Qur'ān states: "O People of the Scriptures, come to an agreement between us and you that we shall worship none but God, and that we shall ascribe no partner unto Him, and that none of us shall take others for lords besides God." (Qur'ān: Sūra 3: 64, 'Imrān)

Muslims are encouraged to strengthen their link with Christians and Jews based on a common religious belief. This belief could provide the good though long overdue basis for better understanding between Muslims and the People of the Book.

Hajji Riadh El-Droubie[8]

We need to appreciate what others believe. But it must be with a real understanding, which does not gloss over the differences. When it is a matter of heaven or hell, of salvation, how can we be indifferent? It is no good saying superficially we are all the same – we are not.

In showing appreciation, there are acts of courtesy that help. For instance, when Muslims are fasting it might be courteous of others not to eat or drink with them for an hour. And Muslims might refrain from serving meat when there are Hindus present.

Enche Uthman al Muhammadi, Department of<br>Islamic Studies, University of Malaya[9]

The different religions are like a tree. There is one root and many branches. On each branch there is a light, and the lights are of differing colours. But they all draw their light from the one root.

We all need to keep our own light bright.

Sayyeda Fatima al-Yashrutiyya[10]

Belief in One God brings us to believe in the oneness of mankind. On the unity of mankind is built the concept of human brotherhood. This brotherhood includes all who believe in God, whether Jews, Christians or Muslims. These are "The People of the Book".

But this excludes those who are not believers in God. This is a challenge to Islam, to broaden its concept of human brotherhood to include believers and non-believers.

Muslim mystics have been the forerunners of such a broadening. The famous mystic Ibn al-Arabi, for instance, says that his brother is the other man, regardless of his religion, race or colour.

Dr Hassan Saab[11]

The spirit of Islam is a wonderful thing, but it is forgotten even in Islam itself.

We need bridges, give and take, between religions. They should be fellows in a common task, but each pretends that absolute truth belongs only to itself, and that the others are invaders. All have had an attitude which is ungenerous and irreligious. It has cut away common actions for the same aims, for centuries.

About 1890, an Armenian came to a mosque and asked for guidance. He was one of a community that lived closely with Muslims. He was directed to a certain Shaikh who taught him, and whom he greatly respected. After a while he said, "I have decided to become a Muslim. I find your teaching and life better than that of our Christian people." The Shaikh said, "If you do this, I will never give you my hand again, nor teach you. There is no need to change your religion to become a better man. Think of your family and the division you will cause."

Ahmet Emin Yalman[12]

Tile inscribed with *ḥadīth*: "The Prophet said:
The intention is the act. Conferences call for integrity,
security for discretion ..."  Iran, 1263 AD

## The Crusades

The memory of the Crusades still has an embittering effect on Muslim-Christian relations. In the past there has been much mutual recrimination: counter-accusations of the rack and the sword, of responsibility for wars of conquest in the Seventh Century, and world conflicts in the Twentieth.

A talk took place between a number of leading Muslim political figures in Iran and the holder of a proud and ancient French name whose ancestors were Crusaders. This French gentleman said: "My ancestors took part in the Crusades. My family have always been very proud of their prowess in arms, and courage. But I have come to realise how far it was from the teachings of my Lord and God to set out to enforce the Will of the Prince of Peace by arms and weapons. It was not His way. It was not the way of St Francis of Assisi with your Muslim leaders. I would like to make what restitution can be made after eight hundred years. I am sorry for our misconceptions then, for our family pride in them, and for all the consequences this has had for the world."

The Muslims present were deeply moved. The Prime Minister, Dr Matine Daftary, rose to his feet and said:

None of us ever expected to hear such words from any of you. We do not want anything of you except the practice of the teaching of your Master. One saying of his, "Turn the other cheek," if you put it into practice, would transform the world and draw us all to you.[13]

# "City of Wrong": A Muslim Study of the Crucifixion

A study in depth of the Crucifixion by a Muslim is something new. Dr Kamil Hussein was awarded the State Prize for Literature for his book *City of Wrong* when it appeared in Cairo in 1957.

In it the author, a doctor and a devout Muslim scholar, paints an artist's portrait of Jerusalem on the first Good Friday, and explores the implication of the fact that men like ourselves were ready to do away with Jesus. "From the point of view of human involvement the crime was accomplished when Christ was condemned to death," he says. "The fact that God raised him to Himself in no way mitigates the iniquity of what was done."[14] For while no Muslim believes that Jesus was actually crucified, they hold that it was God's intervention that prevented this when men had decided to perpetrate the outrage. The key passage in the Qur'ān is: "They (the Jews) say 'We killed Christ the son of Mary, the Apostle of God': but they killed him not, nor crucified him. But so it was made to appear to them ... Nay, God raised him up unto Himself." (Qur'ān: Sūra 4: 157 *Women*)

*City of Wrong* is fictional in form. It takes each of the actors in the drama of Good Friday and sensitively explores the motives, the attitudes, the struggles with conscience which led them to justify what they did – or to take to their heels and run.

The whole book is a plea for the rule of human conscience, and for the rejection of the thesis that the individual conscience can be salved by the doubtful necessity of safeguarding the interests of others. "The wrong was only carried through by dint of being parcelled out among a large number of people, so that no single individual had any longer to think of himself as personally responsible."[15]

The book begins as follows:

The day was a Friday.

But it was quite unlike any other day.

It was a day when men went very grievously astray, so far astray in fact that they involved themselves in the utmost iniquity ...

Yet for all that they were people of religion and character and the most careful of men about following the right ...

On that day men willed to murder their conscience, and that decision constitutes the supreme tragedy of humanity. That day's deeds are a revelation of all that drives men into sin. No evil has ever happened which does not originate in this will of men to slay their conscience and extinguish its light, while they take their guidance from elsewhere. There is no evil afflicting humanity which does not derive from this besetting desire to ignore the dictates of conscience.

The events of that day do not simply belong to the annals of the early centuries. They are disasters renewed daily in the life of every individual. Men to the end of time will be contemporaries of that memorable day, perpetually in danger of the same sin and wrongdoing into which the inhabitants of Jerusalem then fell. The same darkness will be theirs until they are resolute not to transgress the bounds of conscience.[16]

## God Knows the Thoughts of Men

In Westminster Abbey, 1 June 1973, at "An Observance for Commonwealth Day", representatives of Islam made their contributions together with those of other faiths. The passage chosen from the Qur'ān, and read by H.E. The High Commissioner for Nigeria in London, was the opening of Sūra 57 (*Iron*):

In the Name of Allah, the Compassionate, the Merciful.
All that is in heaven and earth gives glory to Allah. He is the Mighty, the Wise One.

His is the kingdom of the heavens and the earth. He ordains life and death and has power over all things.

He is the first and the last, the visible and the unseen. He has knowledge of all things.

He created the heavens and the earth in six days and then mounted His throne. He knows all that goes into the earth and all that emerges from it, all that comes down from heaven and all that ascends to it. He is with you wherever you are. Allah is cognizant of all your actions.

His is the kingdom of the heavens and the earth. To Him shall all things return. He causes the night to pass into the day and the day into the night. He has knowledge of the inmost thoughts of men.

# CHAPTER TWELVE

## *The Bridge from Death to Life*

He who has done an atom's weight of
good shall see it; and he who has done
an atom's weight of evil shall see it.

Qur'ān: Sūra 99: 7–8 *The Earthquake*

Said Jesus (on whom be peace): 'The
world is a bridge. Therefore cross it;
do not dwell on it.'

Tradition, quoted by Al-Ghazali, and
inscribed by the Emperor Akbar
on the gate of Fatehpur Sikri[1]

My soul, like a homing bird, yearning
   for paradise,
Shall arise and soar, from the snares of
   the world set free
When the voice of Thy love shall call
   me.

From the tomb of the poet Hafiz, Shiraz[2]

# The Bridge of Death

What does the Muslim expect to follow death?

The passer-by, reading the funeral notices posted outside a mosque, finds them couched in terms of the Qur'ānic verse:

> Thou soul at peace
> Return unto thy Lord, content in His good pleasure.
> Enter thou among My servants.
> Enter thou My garden.
>
> Qur'ān: Sūra 89: 27–30 *Daybreak*

In facing death, and in moments of sore bereavement, the Qur'ān has much to offer of comfort and strength. The customary greeting at such times is, "May He pour out on you patience and consolation." On graves centuries old, as well as those of today, are the words: "We are God's and to Him we return." On war memorials we read:

> Think not of those who are slain in the way of Allah, as dead.
> Nay, they are living. With their Lord they have provision.
>
> Qur'ān: Sūra 3: 169 *'Imrān*

At a memorial meeting in Delhi in honour of the late President of India, Dr Zakir Hussain, the passage read was a famous one which expresses the change from restriction to freedom, hardship to ease.

> Have we not . . . eased thee of the burden
> Which weighed down thy back;
> And exalted thy fame?
>
> But lo! with hardship goeth ease.
> Lo! with hardship goeth ease.
> So when thou art relieved, still toil
> And strive to please thy Lord.
>
> Qur'ān: Sūra 94: 1–8 *Solace*

After death, there is hope of joy – and certainty of judgment. Dr Azzam says, "The prophet fired his Message with every resource of language and metaphor until it seared the ears of his people. And then he told them of the last day when a just reckoning would be taken of the deeds they had done, and he spoke of Paradise and Hell with all the glow of Eastern imagery."[3] The mental images he used to express the inexpressible differ from those of the Book of Revelation, with its pearly gates and streets of gold. The burning desert is the background, and against it springs the vivid green where water brings life-giving growth. Paradise is a garden where drink does not intoxicate,[4] and where women are pure and modest. According to the Qur'ān, men and women are admitted on the same terms. Fathers, mothers and children enter Paradise together:[5]

> Allah has promised to the believing men and to the believing women Gardens in which rivers flow, to abide in them, and goodly dwellings in Gardens of perpetual abode: and the greatest of all is Allah's good pleasure – that is the grand achievement.
>
> Qur'ān: Sūra 9: 72 *Repentance*

> Their cry in it shall be glory to Thee, O Allah!
> And their greeting in it shall be, Peace!
>
> Qur'ān: Sūra 10: 10 *Jonah*

There is nothing wrong to the Muslim mind if the women in Paradise are said to be beautiful. It is the western critic, he feels, who consistently sees these pictures in terms of sex. Moreover, not all agree with modern attempts to explain away the realities of Paradise and Hell. To an American writer one cultured Muslim said:

> Today much effort is being spent to prove that Muḥammad's paradise was only symbolic. Wise men explain away everything. But let me tell you this. I have lived my life faithful to God in this baking desert. I have avoided one earthly temptation after another in an effort to gain paradise. If I get there and find no cool rivers, no date trees and no beautiful girls . . . to keep me company, I shall feel badly defrauded.[6]

## A Pilgrim's Prayer

O God, make the end of my life the best of my life,
And the best of my deeds, their conclusion,
And the best of my days, the day on which I shall meet Thee.

O God, make death the best of those things we choose not,
But which we await;
And the grave the best dwelling in which we shall dwell –
And, than death, make best that which follows death.[7]

# A War-time Letter of Condolence

Following the Arab-Israeli hostilities of October 1973, a poignant exchange of letters took place between Mrs Jehanne Sadat, wife of President Sadat, and Mrs Ophira Telem of Acre. Mrs Telem wrote to Mrs Sadat asking her help to recover the body of her brother, an Israeli frogman who was killed in a commando operation off Port Said. She described the grief of her mother and father, and the sympathy expressed to them by many Arab friends. "We have no grudge against the Arabs," she said, and described how as a teacher she had prevented her pupils from writing anti-Arab sentiments in essays.

Mrs Sadat's reply expressed her condolences to Mrs Telem, and to the boy's mother and relatives. Her own family too, she said, mourned a similar loss, for the President's brother, an air pilot, was killed on the first day of the war:

> I paid much attention to your request to find out the fate of your brother. I discovered that our forces did not find his body, because the ocean waves carried him far out after he had attacked the shores of Port Said as a frogman.
>
> Your mother's feelings touch my heart – because I too am a mother, and because I have met many mothers and fathers in my country who lost their children during the war . . . I beg God that He make up the loss of her son by a future in which she will live in peace.
>
> In every soldier who fell in the War of the Tenth of Ramaḍān, there is our son and part of our soul. I want to emphasise to you and to anyone who reads this letter that we are sincere in every step we take towards a real, just and lasting peace. We want to build and develop, we want our people to realise the hope of a happy family and a happy home.
>
> Wars know no real victor, no real vanquished. The losses hit both sides, the price is enormous and painful. It is the sacrifice of thousands of young people, the mourning and grief in the hearts of the mothers, the wives, the fathers. Our hearts are pained to the depths by the loss of one young person, of one child.
>
> Such grief as yours is the result of war, which we try in every way to prevent, to open the doors to peace so that no one will have to face the horrors caused by the loss of young men on both sides.[8]

# CHAPTER THIRTEEN

## *The Bridge from Youth to Faith*

To make factories and high buildings is
easy. To build man, that is the difficult
thing. Returning to God is an essential
way to achieve the good man and the
good society.

Student leader, Cairo[1]

We long to build lasting, reliable
bridges with the strength of pre-
stressed concrete. They must have the
steel bars of absolute standards – no
bubbles or cracks to rust the steel. Our
personal change is the pre-stressing
process. Then we can carry the loads
that must pass over these bridges.

Student of architecture, Cairo[2]

The future of any faith depends on its ability to capture one generation after another. Each in succession has to bridge the gap between man and God for itself.

Some trends of the day militate against faith and tradition: others towards a whole-hearted acceptance of them. Many of the younger generation express a loyalty to their faith which shapes their family relationships, their choice of career, their political views, their dreams for the future. In this highly sensitive area of understanding generalisations are dangerous. Under the surface unexpected currents flow. Students from British universities visiting Egypt, for instance, comment with respect on the clarity with which their hosts have expressed their beliefs, on their sense of responsibility for the present as well as the future of their country, and also on their readiness for co-operation with others on the basis of similar ideals.[3]

The student population of the Muslim world, as elsewhere is growing in numbers and influence. New universities are opened, while thousands of young men and women are sent to study abroad, the majority to Europe and America. Strident voices summon them to this or that ideology, or experiment in permissiveness: calls which may enlist, confuse or corrupt them. They listen – but how far do they respond?

Among students and young professional men and women, many are to be found who will talk openly and honestly about what they believe and practise. Two of these, quoted in the following pages, represent between them some of the pressures brought to bear on their generation. One studied near home, in Ankara, and was involved in strikes which closed her university. The other was sent by her family from Iran to study music in Geneva, in an environment totally strange to her. Each in her own way has found the road to faith. What they say throws light on the needs and longings of thousands of others, at home or in the west.

## The Hunger for Faith

A student of science was sent home while her university was closed owing to strikes in which she had taken an active part. It was at this time that her search for faith began.

Faith is not an abstract concept. People have not searched through the ages merely for a definition. What do they look for? What did I look for?

Sometimes I did not know what I was looking for. But I knew certain things – maybe I knew what was lacking.

I knew that I was discontented with myself and with what I was living for. I felt that the targets for my life were never big enough or deep enough – they only amounted to my own satisfaction and my own future. Also I knew that there were many wrong things happening around me and in me – cheating, corruption, exploitation. I did not know how one could even start to cure such wrongs, so I was highly cynical.

These things made me look for a faith. Then I saw that God gives the opportunity to acquire faith. It is up to me to choose to want it; and also, once I want it, to work for it.

How does one build and strengthen faith?

Surrendering my will and life to what I know and believe of God. That is the start.

Discipline in finding His way, and obeying Him.

Giving what I have discovered of faith to others.

The faith that we hunger for is something that is inviolable, unshaken by wars or by worries, by corruption or by pressure from outside on our minds and on our hearts.

It is something that is not man-made, but which bridges or surpasses all the divisions that are man-made: divisions of class, of way of life, of riches and poverty, colour and race.

It is something that demands of us the truest and the best; and which promises us the truest and the best.

I need faith – where I am bound to fail – for myself, for others and for my nation. All ideologies take faith, and all revolutions take a lot of faith. But some rely on men and do not demand everything. The faith I speak of asks for everything and depends on God.

Çiğdem Bilginer, Turkey[4]

# The Generation Gap

A gifted young pianist from Iran found that the transition to a strange environment accentuates the generation gap, and threatens a loss of identity that can lead to much confusion and unhappiness. But through her experiences she found the road to a life purpose.

When I lived in Iran, I had a strong faith. When I came to Europe, I was too shy to stand for what is right, and I gradually lost my faith. People who know a lot, I thought, do not need God, and I wanted to be one of them. But sometimes I felt very confused. Ideas went round and round in my head, and when I could not sleep I felt a need to write down these thoughts of mine, to find out what brought me to such a state.

Sometimes I felt a strong need to pray, but intellectually I could not believe that God was there. When for the first time I heard people saying that God can speak to you, I thought that such an inner voice was part of myself. But very slowly I began to know God, as a Power beyond myself. In Iran, I believed in Him and asked Him what *I* wanted, but this time I tried to find out what *He* wanted from me.

How simple it was to seek God's direction – yet I had made it so complicated. It calls for a clear mind, without daydreams and wandering imagination. So I found the need to compare my life daily with God-given standards of right and wrong. I see it like this. A ship at sea needs a compass to steer by, otherwise it goes off course. In the same way, I need absolute moral standards, to know where I am going in life and to be effective on my way. As I try to live by these standards I am learning to distinguish between God's will and my personal wishes.

We young people are very ready to criticise the establishment or our parents, but we refuse to take the blame when we are wrong ourselves. The reason why there is a generation gap is that we are simply too cowardly to accept what we are really like. We criticise our parents, and they criticise us, and we never find an answer to fill the gap.

When I reached a certain age, I started feeling superior to my mother, and often hurt her. Her advice seemed old-fashioned, so I did exactly what I wanted. One day I broke through my pride and apologised. It was as though the two sides of the gap were sewn together. I felt that suddenly my mother had become a close friend. I know that it is not the same for all young people. It is not always we who are wrong. But if we have the courage to give up *our* weaknesses, we can help others find a way for theirs.

There is a gap between young people and faith today because they say that God and moral values have failed to give an answer to humanity. I think it is man who has failed, in refusing to carry moral standards into action. The hate which brings war and division is only a multiplication of the hate we ourselves have against someone. Man has had a stomach too large and eyes too wide – but a heart too small and a spirit too narrow. God's creation has made him think of what he can get out of it, rather than what he can give in order to complete it.

Each of us is meant to be a force and to find self realisation through what we do in our lifetime. So why not master our weaknesses and find fulfilment – in order to save the world? This is the only answer I see for our world today.

Taraneh Azima-Kayhan, Iran[5]

Multi-level patterns are often composed of independent designs.
This is one of three used in one carpet.

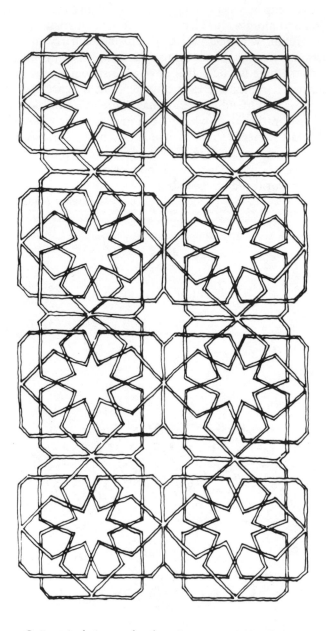

Geometric design used as base in contemporary carpet,
and combined with the arabesque pattern on page 137

# PART FOUR
*The Road to Knowledge*

# CHAPTER FOURTEEN

# *A Philosophy for Education*

The Muslim educator should think
again and evaluate his actual position.
On the one hand, he should uphold his
Islamic heritage and Islamic identity;
on the other, he should adopt from
the West elements of human welfare,
power, science, industry and organiz-
ation. He should beware of distortion
of his national and religious identity,
and of the mistakes and ills with which
the West is now afflicted.

Dr Fadhel Jamali[1]

One of the boys at the Mullah's
school asked a trick question: What
is man's greatest achievement? 'I
don't know about all that,' said the
Mullah, 'but I do know a more difficult task than any – trying to teach
you to see things as they really are.'

Idries Shah[2]

How to combine the necessary equipment for life in the Twentieth Century with the character values and beliefs of Islam: this is a question facing every Muslim country today.

From the first days of Islam, education has had a high priority. Great importance has been attached to the search for knowledge of God's creation and to the care of children from the earliest age. The range of philosophy and practice is vast.

From Tunis comes a series of books outlining a modern philosophy of education. The author is Dr Mohammad Fadhel Jamali, Professor of the Philosophy of Education in the University of Tunis.

Dr Jamali started as a teacher in his native Iraq, but then moved into politics. During the 1950's he was at different times Prime Minister and Foreign Minister, and he often represented his country at the United Nations as well as in the developments in Afro-Asian co-operation that led to the conference in Bandung in 1955. His influence there was exerted in favour of a neutral, rather than an anti-western, stand.

After the Iraqi revolution of 1958 he was held in prison under sentence of death. For eighteen months he did not know from one night to the next when the sentence would be carried out. During that time, he says, he read through the whole Qur'ān over thirty times. He wrote a series of letters to his son, pouring out his convictions about Islam and its relevance to the problems that confronted him as a man and as a statesman. The censor used to read these letters aloud to interested officers, and then forward them. They were afterwards published.[3]

When he was released in 1961, President Bourguiba invited him to Tunisia, where he returned to his original profession. Education, as he sees it, is the most important aspect of development in Muslim countries today. After the widespread struggle for independence, it is the next focus of growth. It depends above all on the quality of the men and women who teach – and it is for them that he writes.

The first book in the series, *The Education of the New Man*[4], appeared in 1967. It traces the development of educational thought from Plato and Aristotle to the Qur'ān, and assesses its educational philosophy. Dr Jamali goes on to consider the character training necessary to equip the "new type of man" called for in the modern world.

In *Horizons of the New Education in the Developing Countries*[5] he turns to the key role played by education in national growth.

In *Towards a Unity of Educational Thought in the Islamic World*[6] he sums up the present situation in regard to education in the Muslim world.

## The Character of the "New Man"

The greatest need in the developing countries is the development of a "new man". Men are needed who will give the best of which they are capable, undeterred by apathy or ambition, discouragement or danger.

The "new man" will need new characteristics, and the educator can shape his work to produce them.

First, integrity. Personal integrity must lead to a wholeness of character in which narrow partisanship can be banished without curbing individual freedom of thought. Man's many-sided nature must be developed, with special regard to aspects in which our world today may be reckoned backward – the moral and spiritual potentialities that distinguish men from beasts.

Next, emotional control. The results of unbridled hate and greed and domination are to be seen everywhere, and retard human progress. Control of the right kind leaves room for the love of truth to grow. It must be the *whole* truth, and that not merely in a scientific sense. Truth is as greatly needed in human relationships. When there is so much to mislead and divide, a passion for truth is needed which will detect falsehood and free people to be in a right relation to each other. Here the teacher's own attitude counts more than anything else. Only those who have been set free can free others. Only the loved can love.

School life can make it clear that position of any sort is an opportunity for service, not self-advancement. It can also foster the kind of responsibility that sees things through – for lack of which so many good projects fail. Class divisions, as well as national antagonisms, must be counteracted.

To bring out man's essential humanity is the aim. Intelligence and conscience are the pinnacle of evolution. There is a Higher Intelligence and purpose at work in the universe, and perception of this brings a belief in God which is not servile (as it may sometimes have been in the past) but is the result of a deliberate decision.

Faith, profound and sincere, is the highest aim of the educator.

Dr Fadhel Jamali, *The Education of the New Man*[7]

# A Constructive Revolution

The past years have been marked by a struggle for independence, which has overshadowed everything else in the developing nations. Emerging from this, they find their next focus of growth in questions of education. This is a major concern for the leaders of nations.

This century has seen different types of revolution – most of them involving violence and bloodshed. Changing the form of government does not necessarily achieve the basic revolution that is sought. There is no magic wand for progress. It has to deal with the character of men.

It is true to say that any positive revolution, whether it concerns politics, material progress or economics, cannot succeed unless it is accompanied by a revolution in character. While greed and selfishness persist, while favouritism and bribery are widespread, while honesty is lacking and a sense of duty is weak, there is no hope of success.

An authentic revolution must be preceded and accompanied by a moral revolution based on absolute honesty, absolute unselfishness, absolute purity and absolute love. The educator must boldly undertake this revolution of character, for without it no sound revolution can start, and if it does start it will not continue.

It is the business of the new education to bring about a constructive revolution.

Dr Fadhel Jamali, *Horizons of the New*
*Education in the Developing Countries*[8]

# Towards a Unity of Educational Thought in the Islamic World

Since World War II over thirty countries with a Muslim majority have become independent. All of them belong to the newly awakened Third World, which has only recently taken the road to development and prosperity. The new governments have with great energy started modern schools on a western model. The old schools in their inherited form were inadequate to meet the needs of a contemporary age – a great tragedy. But the new ones are neglecting the traditional virtues of religion and character, and are thereby endangering their national and Islamic identity – the loss of which would be a greater calamity.

143

For this reason the Muslim world today faces a crisis in regard to education. Muslim teachers need a new educational philosophy: one which will bring about a renaissance among the peoples of Islam – a renaissance that is scientific, social and economic as well as spiritual and moral. Such a renaissance calls for thought and action in the following directions.

1. A profound study of the Islamic system of belief, the sources of its strength and vitality, in order to build the new education on these points of strength.
2. A study of the factors making for backwardness in the Islamic world. It must be recognised that Islam is not only *not* responsible for this backwardness, but actually proscribes it. We can be satisfied that backwardness is mainly caused by moral disease.
3. A study of the educational system of western origin – its strong and weak points: and also of the educational philosophy found in the Holy Qur'ān. This, in our opinion, is more comprehensive and complete than any western philosophy we know.
4. A confrontation with the challenges which western creeds present to us, in the name of humanism and democracy.
5. A recognition by Muslim educators of the need to revive the Islamic identity by their teaching. This they can do by teaching Muslims the truth of their religion, and also the practice of it, and by developing feelings of brotherhood and unity between Muslims. Also, they need to have a regard for the Arabic language. This, as the language of the Holy Qur'ān, belongs to all Muslims, as well as being the national tongue of the Arabs.

In the present phase of the struggle between good and evil, there is a real danger that mankind may be destroyed. The Muslim teacher, armed with a sound philosophy, can play a valuable part in ensuring world survival and achieving world peace.

Dr Fadhel Jamali, *Towards a Unity of Educational Thought*[9]

# CHAPTER FIFTEEN

## *Advance and Reform*

We must find again the unprejudiced and receptive mind of the early days of Islam, so that we are capable of meeting the fast-changing challenges of the time and contributing fully to the enrichment of the heritage of mankind as a whole.

Mohammed Wahby[1]

The teacher's faith in God is his invaluable asset. It is his binding duty to inculcate the love of God in the hearts of his pupils, as an inexhaustible source of nobility of character.

Teachers' Charter of Honour,
Egyptian Teachers Syndicate[2]

The phenomenon of a pluralistic society which today confronts Britain and many other countries, East and West, is not something new in man's history. The cross-fertilisation of ideas, cultures and races has been a major force in the development of human civilisation.

Muslim Guide, Islamic Foundation, Leicester[3]

In Muslim countries educational institutions vary from the simplest Qur'ānic school teaching Arabic letters to African and Asian children, to the great universities of Cairo and other capitals.

Modern national systems of education have been developed by Arab and other governments in the course of this century.

Alongside these are flourishing colleges specifically Muslim in foundation. Examples of great Islamic establishments dedicated to education could be given from India and Indonesia, Malaysia and Sri Lanka, as well as Pakistan, Nigeria and the Arab states, and more recently in western countries.

The less able, whether mentally retarded or otherwise handicapped, are also cared for, since "In the sight of Islam, education concerns the human being taken as a whole, whatever may be his natural gifts and abilities."[4]

Most famous of all Islamic educational institutions is the University of Al-Azhar in Cairo. The issues faced in connection with the reform and expansion of this ancient seat of learning in the 1960's are discussed in this section. So also are some of the educational questions that arise in Britain's Muslim community.


## The Reform of Al-Azhar

The oldest university in the world is Al-Azhar, in Cairo. In AD 969 a coup took place by which the Fatimids ousted the representatives of the Abbasid caliphs and took over Egypt. The Fatimid general laid out a new capital city, which was built while he restored law and order to the plague-stricken, famished populace. Just inside the walls he built the spacious colonnades of Al-Azhar mosque. Within a few years it became a school of higher studies, as it has been ever since.

Al-Azhar, as the acknowledged intellectual centre of Islam, has for centuries conserved its faith, its law and its language. Here, through good times and bad, have been trained the men who have transmitted these things in faithful detail throughout the growing extent of the Muslim world. In the steady peaceful expansion of Islam into Asia and Africa, merchants and Sufis took the faith, and Azharis consolidated it. From early times a scholarship system has supported young men from many countries, and today the hostels of Al-Azhar house students from every continent. Muslim families from Africa and the Far East, as well as from Egypt itself, were and are proud to send one son to study there.

In its ancient courts one is transported back in history to mediaeval ways of learning. White-turbaned shaikhs sit by the pillars, text in hand, the students squatting round them. Blind scholars cultivate the retentive memory that will ensure an accurate recital of every syllable of the Qur'ān in faraway mosques for years to come. But a busy modern university lies behind these graceful porticos. Nearby are the buildings which arose after the reforms of Mohammed Abduh at the beginning of the century, and further away on the edge of the desert are the hostels and laboratories of the modern faculties.

After the Egyptian revolution of 1952, it was decided to modernise Al-Azhar, and to introduce new faculties of medicine, engineering, commerce and agriculture – and also a college for women. By 1979, the numbers of men had expanded to 33,000, and new universities had been established on the same pattern in a number of Egyptian centres.

The perspective in which this transformation took place is set out in the Preamble to the new constitution:

> For centuries Al-Azhar has played a great role in the history of science, and in that of Islam, as also in our national struggle [in Egypt]. Like a mighty fortress, it has opposed all attempts at imposing outside domination.
>
> But with this opposition has grown a certain conservatism. Azharis have been regarded – and have regarded themselves – as men of religion, with little to do with the sciences of this world. Islam, according to its true nature, does not make any such distinction. Every Muslim ought to be at the same time a "man of religion" and a "man of the world".
>
> Today the Muslim world is expanding, and its intellectual horizons are widening. . . . In many recently liberated countries, programmes are established in the realm of industry, commerce, mines, education, public health and other fields of national advance. In practice, specialists in these fields are usually strangers to the religion and customs of the country, whether they be its citizens or foreigners. Fellow compatriots who have both professional competence and a live religious faith have to be searched for, and it is hard to know where to send people so that they may acquire experience, knowledge and faith – three indispensable qualities if these countries are to achieve renaissance and follow the right road. Many sent abroad with scholarships return with

professional qualifications but knowing nothing of their religion. In contrast, those with scholarships at Al-Azhar return having learned a great deal about the Qur'ān, but they have no trade and cannot participate in the national advance. Through both groups, social life is complicated and the advance is retarded ... Institutes of Higher Islamic Studies should therefore add other teaching to their religious studies. When their studies are completed, these students will hold key positions in every sphere of activity.[5]

## Al-Azhar in Action

The man entrusted with the framing of a new policy for Al-Azhar was Shaikh Ahmad Hassan al-Baqoury, who was appointed Minister of Waqfs (Religious Foundations) in 1952. In conversation with the writer (1969) he stressed the importance of the reforms for Egypt, for the rest of the Muslim world, and for Muslim-Christian relations. His invitation to Cardinal Koenig to lecture in Al-Azhar was one example of his concern for these relations.[6]

He also gave me the unusual privilege of attending a session of the University Council. Round the long table were seated the Deans of the Faculties, ranging from the most venerable of shaikhs to the modern scientists, and including the most revolutionary figure of all – the Principal of the Women's College which now forms part of Al-Azhar. The Rector presided with wisdom and humour. The care given to the needs of individual students was impressive. The welfare of the Palestinian students, postgraduate courses for those from Malaysia, the examination for a doctorate of an eminent Jordanian, were typical cases. A shaikh raised the question as to whether the students of engineering were all receiving religious education. (Each student takes a course in Islamics and Arabic, in which he must pass every year, along with his professional studies.) The qualifications for entering Al-Azhar were on the agenda. There are schools under the same foundation which give boys an education in Qur'ānic studies, alongside a modern curriculum. Some wished to narrow the university intake to these schools, but the representative of the Ministry of Higher Education protested. A list of applicants for post-graduate studies included students with qualifications from Islamic colleges in Pakistan, Baghdad, Damascus and Indonesia. The point at issue was the unique status of Al-Azhar and its responsibility for setting standards throughout the Muslim world.

One historic change was the re-introduction of Shī'ī studies to Al-

Azhar. It was the Ayyubid ruler Salāḥ al-dīn (Saladin, d AD 1193) who changed its basis from the original Shī'ism of the Fatimids. For nearly 800 years the Ja'afarī school of law recognised by the Shī'īs was excluded. From 1953 it became a recognised subject of study alongside the four Sunni schools, (Ḥanafī, Mālikī, Shāfi'ī and Ḥanbalī).

Many feel that the hopes of the reformers were misplaced, and that the expansion of Al-Azhar took place at the expense of traditional standards of scholarship. Shaikh Baqoury himself foresaw the difficulties. "The changes will not happen quickly," he said. "They will take a generation. We are fighting a battle against materialism, and it will be a long one."[7]

The need remains both for leadership in different spheres of public life, and for the highest standards of Qur'ānic scholarship. The debate continues as to how both these needs can be served.

Pulpit of Sultan Kait Bey
Cairo, 15th century AD

## The Women of Al-Azhar

The education of women in the Muslim world made rapid strides during the 1950's and 1960's. For the highest religious authorities to offer women an education equal to that of men, in the traditional stronghold of Al-Azhar, was one outstanding innovation.

The task of creating the new Women's College was entrusted to Dr Zeinab Rashed in 1962. She is an historian, with a Ph.D from the University of Liverpool, for a book on the Peace of Paris. Later she became a trusted adviser in the development of education for girls in Saudi Arabia.

Under her guidance the Women's College of Al-Azhar quickly drew girls from many Muslim countries, as well as thousands of young Egyptians, taking a wide variety of courses. The first of its new buildings was made possible by a gift from Kuwait. In 1979, the numbers of students had risen to over 11,000. In 1988 there were 23,000 women in eight colleges associated with Al-Azhar, in Cairo, Alexandria, Asyut and elsewhere.

The scope of the influence of the Women's College was already apparent to a visitor during its formative years. In one room was a class in thermo-dynamics, taught by an Egyptian graduate of Leeds University: in another, a number of girls were waiting their turn to take part in a competition for recitation of the Qur'ān. For the medical course, there were picked students from many Arab countries. Most of those who came from Asia and Africa took specialised courses in Arabic and Islamics, with a view to teaching in their home countries.

Dr Zeinab spoke of the aims of herself and her colleagues:

> The great question in my mind is the framing of character. Religious education such as we give forms a certain type of personality – responsible, stable: people who work efficiently whatever their profession, who understand that religion is not just for paradise, but is a question of living now. We do get results along this line – not a hundred per cent, of course, but even if twenty-five per cent of our girls fully accept such aims I feel it will make a real contribution.[8]

The doctor in charge of the Women's Medical Faculty added:

> For centuries religion has been thought a handicap to progress, instead of marching hand in hand with it. We aim to prove that it is an asset, and produces a better quality of scientist. Science aims to make mankind happy, and whether it does so or not depends on the scientist. He or she can affect the way in which technical progress is used, for welfare or destruction.[9]

# Doubt and Certainty

The modernisation of Al-Azhar and the creation of institutions on western models come in for much criticism. Neither, the critics say, succeeds in solving the dilemma which the clash of two cultures poses for the individual. Can an attempt at synthesis succeed? Has Islam, in its wholeness and universality, a distinctive contribution to make in view of the compartmentalism and secularism of modern thought?

Professor Syed Muhammad al-Naquib al-Attas, Dean of the Faculty of Arts in the National University of Malaysia, says:

A different conception of knowledge is necessary, and a different purpose for education.

In Islam the end of knowledge is God; knowledge is not just for secular purposes. Knowledge is one whole. The universe is a book that reveals the Author. Knowledge, if it be true, confirms and affirms God. Thus, knowledge includes faith. This was the conception of knowledge which Al-Azhar originally disseminated. But modern universities have become engrossed in the pursuit of particulars, and have strayed away from the purpose for which universities are formed. The university, as its name implies, must reflect the universal in knowledge; it must not merely involve itself solely in the analytical method while yet losing sight of the synthetical purpose for which analysis can become meaningful. In striving after synthesis the university reflects the universal.

The purpose of education in Islam is the emergence of the complete man. In the West, it is the production of the complete citizen. In Islam, the aim or final purpose for knowing is God. In humanism, the aim is the affirmation of man. This leads to the problem of the West. People are not happy. There is no certainty any longer. People are always seeking – but without the desire or the intention to find. Doubt has gone too far in that it has been raised to the scientific rank in enquiry. Everything is called in question. Doubt is not a reliable method of enquiry.

There must come a swing away from the compartmentalism and one-sidedness of over-specialisation, and towards the wholeness and universality of knowledge: an emphasis again on big things instead of small, ideas rather than mere details.[10]

# Muslims in Britain – Educational Issues

The presence of Muslims in Europe has a long history, full of contrasts. When crusading rhetoric was denouncing them as enemies in distant lands, nearer home in Southern Europe they were respected as masters of philosophy, medicine and mathematics. When the Ottoman civilisation dominated much of Eastern Europe it was admired as well as feared. The buildings and abstract art of Muslim Spain and Egypt influenced Nineteenth Century architects. The period of Empire brought to Europe numbers of students and professional men and women from Muslim countries and from the South Asian subcontinent.

A new chapter has opened in the second half of the twentieth century, with large numbers of Muslims resident in Northern Europe. This offers a challenge to both host populations and immigrants.

In a lecture *Islam in Britain* (1981), Dr Zaki Badawi, Principal of the Muslim College, Ealing, and former Director of the Islamic Cultural Centre, London, described the Muslims in Britain, about 1½ million strong, as "a community of great vitality and talent . . . struggling to earn a living in unfamiliar surroundings", and in its present form "only about two decades old."[11] It was the shortage of manpower in the industries of Britain in the 1950's and 1960's that brought large numbers from Pakistan, India and later Bangladesh to work in Yorkshire textile mills and foundries, in Midland industries and in Greater London. There was scope too for small enterprises and shopkeepers. The adjustments for uneducated workers were difficult, and when recession threatened they encountered hostility from some of the host community who were themselves undergoing much hardship.

Muslims in Britain are of various racial origins, and the first generation speak many languages – Urdu, Gujerati, Bengali, Punjabi and some Arabic. While the majority come from South Asia, some groups come from West Africa and Malaysia, Turkey and Cyprus, South Africa, East Africa and the Caribbean. A few are Arabs – among them some who are wealthy. There are also a number of men and women who have embraced Islam. Such diverse groupings lack effective organisation, and they have no central authority. "The challenges facing Muslims are growing in complexity and they are adapting, albeit slowly, to the new environment," says Doctor Badawi. "They are moving towards integration without assimilation. They are becoming a part of the Great British community without losing their identity as Muslims."[12]

The primary place for this process of assimilation is in school. The Education Act of 1988 focussed important issues in this regard. It was estimated that 350,000 Muslim children – British citizens – were in the state school system, an important segment of the nation's future.

The reactions to the Act were various. Its provision for daily acts of Christian worship, together with the complexity of the regulations for variations to these, or withdrawal of children from them, perturbed many Muslim parents. It is not religious teaching as such to which they object: under the 1944 Act it was rather to the neglect of it, "the frequent misuse of time supposed to be devoted to it, in ways that diminish respect for faith in God of any kind."[13] The Muslim Education Trust, in a letter to the Secretary of State for Education (June 1988), thanked the Department "for all the positive steps taken to strengthen the moral fibre of the multi-faith and multi-cultural society in which we live." At the same time basic educational concerns were voiced, including the right to withdraw children from specifically Christian teaching, and the provision of Islamic education suited to their needs: and that girls of secondary age should be allowed "to wear modest dress and headscarf conforming to the colour of the school uniform."[14] This reflects the constant concern for the education of girls and the preference for separate schools for them at the secondary stage.

A response to the Act came from Riadh El-Droubie, Director of Minaret House and author of books to help the teaching of Islam in schools:

Our belief is that morality and the social values of the society can only be based on a firm faith in God and on religious convictions. . . . Our aim is not to undermine the teaching of Christianity in schools. We accept the fact that it is the predominant faith of this country. However it should be recognised that Britain today is a multi-cultural and multi-faith society. It is our firm conviction that no believer should be expected to take part in an act of worship which indicates commitment to another faith, therefore each religious community should have the right to its own religious education.[15]

Three tendencies arise in Muslim circles, says Dr Badawi:

What is needed is education *into* the culture of Britain, not outside it. But in cities where the relations with the host community have been difficult, there are people who want to keep the Muslim community apart. They look for separate schools. The majority however want their children to be educated with others, sharing in the national culture and community in which they will live. At the same time, there is a place for some institutions to be set up, specifically based on Islamic principles, and comparable to Catholic and Jewish schools. This is part of the British scene and should be allowed to Muslims as it is to others.[16]

The National Muslim Education Council of the UK, at a conference held in June 1989, stressed the need for more Muslim teachers in state schools, and more Muslim parents as school governors: also that teachers should be trained to give Religious Education to Muslim pupils. To increase the number of dedicated teachers would be one of the greatest contributions the Muslim community could make to its own needs – and to those of the society in which they reside.

Institutions and courses at graduate level are needed to equip Muslims to lead their people in this and other fields. The prospectus of the Muslim College, Ealing, a graduate college developing such courses, gives as its aim training people "able to speak of Islam in terms that the West could easily understand and to guide the community resident here more effectively towards both survival and the making of a positive contribution to the cultures in which they have chosen to live."[17]

Dr Badawi comments:

The generation of Muslims growing up here has to attempt to resolve the ever present tension between the home on the one hand and the school and society at large on the other. They are not unique in this. If we call it a clash of cultures for the immigrant communities we may dignify it with the title of "The Generation Gap" within the local community. . . . The rising generation of Muslims will have no home other than Great Britain and will speak no language with competence other than English. They need to be given a sense of belonging in this country and a sense of acceptability, in contrast to the deep feeling of insecurity many of their parents suffer from.

The Muslim community in Britain, given a sense of security and the circumstances to allow it to remain true to its heritage, can contribute greatly to the cultural life and the economic and social well-being of everyone in this country.[18]

# PART FIVE
*The Journey of the Heart*

# CHAPTER SIXTEEN
## *The Sufi Orders Today*

The heart enquired of the soul
What is the beginning of this business?
What is its end, its fruit?

The soul answered,
The beginning of it is
the annihilation of self.
Its end faithfulness,
and its fruit immortality.

Khawajah Abdullah Ansari[1]

Sufism is the genuine inner life of the
heart.

Fazlur Rahman[2]

Islam is held to be above all a religion of reason. No knowledge lies outside its scope. Its strength lies in the stark simplicity of its creed, and its call for the submission of the will and actions of man to the Will of God. But from the earliest times it has made its appeal to the heart also.

Sufism is the name given to the mysticism of Islam. Its roots are to be traced to very early times. The word probably indicates the wearing of a rough woollen garment as a mark of asceticism. The practice of Sufism developed, however, not in the renunciation of the outer life but in bringing into its every aspect a consciousness of God, and a ceaseless vigil on purity of motive and inner integrity.

The road trodden by the Sufi represents the warm, personal faith that has always been part of the experience of Islam.

The Arabic word for road, ṭarīqa, is used to describe this journey of the heart, and also designates the "ways" or orders formed by those who have banded themselves together to seek such an experience.

These orders have a long, and often controversial, history. Some of Islam's greatest poets have been Sufis, and some of her most brilliant scientists also. The orders have frequently aroused suspicion and opposition, and have been accused of going astray into unorthodox paths. But they are woven into the fabric of Muslim life today, as they have been in the past.


## A New Momentum

Some of the old Sufi orders are at present finding a new momentum. There is a fresh search for reality, especially among the highly educated. Professor Yusuf Ibish, an authority on Sufism as well as a political scientist, comments:

> Most of the traditional orders are still in existence, but their following is not as large as it used to be. They have picked up again in the past decade, I think under the impact of secularism, socialism and all the isms: and of course atheism. Their message is becoming meaningful again to the young. Some orders are gaining membership among the very well educated, and among those who are completely disenchanted with modernism. People are taking a fresh look at Sufism, especially because of its aloofness from politics. Many are tired of meaningless talk about politics and ideologies. There is a return to the essential,

that is God, for the *ṭarīqa* is nothing else than a communal way of searching for the real and attaching oneself to it.

There is very little propaganda. The momentum is gained by a gradual development. Most of the Sufi orders do not want a large following. They think that Sufism is an élite type of affiliation and should remain so. Of course, if the Sufi ideals could be translated into the existing structures of life, all the better.

To those of us who are thinking seriously about the problems of the modern world, Sufism becomes the place where the treasures of man's experience are deposited and preserved. In a storm, one seeks a refuge. If only a few of us survive an atomic blast, we will have preserved a very precious flame. Essentially, Sufism is nothing more and nothing less than making God real in one's heart. This experience must not perish.

Such values always have survived destruction. God is not a dictator in human history, He is a participant. He definitely has an overall plan, however difficult it is for us with our weak and finite insight to understand it. There is a plan, and His Will is worked out eventually.

There is personal discipline, and there is discipline within the order. It has a hierarchy, like all organisations, and there are those who guide others. For example, confronted with a problem I cannot solve, I write to my immediate superior or I meet him and seek an answer from him. Not that I always expect clear-cut, well-defined answers: he may give me guiding principles from the Holy Qur'ān or the sayings of the Prophet, or give me interpretations of his own. If that fails to satisfy my need for an answer, I can write to the highest authority in the organisation. Please do not think in terms of an ecclesiastical order, or oecumenical council. It is highly informal, and on a personal basis. The essential is knowing oneself: discovering one's potential and cultivating that.[3]

# The Mystic Quest is Perennial

An outstanding exponent of Sufism today is Professor Seyyed Hossein Nasr. He writes in English and French, as well as in Arabic and Persian, on a wide range of spiritual and philosophical subjects.

In 1970, he lectured in Australia, at the request of the Charles Strong Trust. Speaking to audiences far removed from his own traditions, he linked certain permanent elements in human personality, including man's constant reaching out to God, with the acute needs of modern, secularised man.

Man was created, says the Qur'ān, "of the best stature", but was reduced to "the lowest of the low". Both aspects are constant in his nature, and he has to find the path that will lead him from the lower to the higher, the path which will allow him to be truly himself. The mystical quest is perennial, because it is part of man's nature. A normal human society is one in which such a quest is given recognition, for without it society will crumble, suffering from psychic maladies it cannot cure.

Both those who wish to fly into space, and those who break the hold of physical sensations upon them by the use of drugs . . . prove through these very efforts the perennity of the mystical quest, in the sense that man, whatever age he lives in, needs the Infinite and Absolute in order to remain man . . . The failure of such efforts, whether space flights or "trips" made possible through drugs – a failure which is instinctively felt by most men to be a poor substitute for that felicity and peace which accompanies all true contacts with the Spirit – itself proves that only a true mysticism that comes from God through one of His revealed religions can make the mystical quest successful. Only a path that comes from God can lead to Him . . .

Sufism is one such path, placed by God within the bosom of Islam in order to provide the possibility of spiritual realisation for the millions of men who over the ages have followed the religion of the Qur'ān . . .

Sufism contains within itself the possibility of being practised in any circumstance in which man finds himself . . . [It] is meant to be practised within society and not in a monastic environment outside the social order. The Sufi bears spiritual poverty (*faqr*) within himself even if he lives outwardly amidst the riches of the world. The world has died in him and he lives in the world without being seduced by it. Sufism is able to integrate man into his Divine Centre wherever he may be, provided he is willing to dedicate himself to the Way, which, being sacred, asks of man all that he is . . .

To the problems of the pathetic lot of modern, secularised man, Sufism would answer by pointing out that man has become miserable only because he no longer knows who he is; and the modern sciences of man as they are usually taught do not aid him one iota in discovering his true identity . . . Sufism sees . . . the desperate attempt on the part of many, for whom the false idols have been broken, to reach the Infinite and the Eternal . . . [It] can turn this urge to follow the mystical way into a wholesome and meaningful direction for those who are willing to accept its discipline or to apply its insights to their own situation.[4]

Lamp engraved on stone
Topkapi Palace, Istanbul, 1464 AD

## Stillness

"Is there communication between God and man?" is a question to which every believing Muslim gives the answer, "Yes". The daily prayers are the framework of it, and to the Sufi the most important part of these prayers comes at the end, says Professor Ibish, "when the worshipper invokes the Divine Name and feels His presence." He continues:

There is no official priesthood in Islam. Communication between God and man can be achieved on a personal basis. If you interpret the rituals of religion – any religion, Islam in particular – in the right way, and cultivate your inner potential, you discover that you need no intermediary. Prayer is an exercise of humility in the Divine presence. This starts right from the point of the ablutions before praying. You start not by cleansing your sin but by washing your face, a simple mark of respect to the person you are going to meet. It is a way of preparing yourself, putting yourself in the atmosphere, or mood, for entering into communion with God.

The cultivation of the spiritual potential in each one of us is vital. Here we should seek the guidance of others. So though there are no official priests, there are others who have had spiritual experience and who have dealt with the mysteries of the self, not in the psychological or psycho-analytical sense but in the spiritual sense. They will guide us and teach us how to develop certain rhythms – the invocation of the Divine Name rhythmically and systematically – whereby we feel we are in the divine presence. What you do rhythmically has a certain influence on the state of your mind and spirit. The shaikh from whom you seek guidance – and any person in whom you have confidence – plays an important role. Like everything else, devotion has to be done with dignity and style. Each person has his style, and finds in his own self how to develop it.

Essentially, devotion is to be able to sit still and do nothing and receive the Divine presence. This is very difficult, there are all kinds of distraction, and many things that pull us away from developing this ability.

The essence is stillness.[5]

# The Law, The Way, The Truth

A picture of a Sufi centre in Iran, that of the Ne'matullahi Sultanali-shahi Sufi Order (shi'ite) in the Gunabad district, is given in a foreword to an outstanding book published in 1966, *A Muslim Commentary on the Universal Declaration of Human Rights*. This study is the work of the leader of the order, Shaikh Sultanhussein Tabandeh. The foreword is written by Abulfazl Hazeghi, on several occasions leader of twenty thousand pilgrims from Iran to Mecca.

On one side of the shrine was erected a *Madrassé*, or Religious School, with rooms and niches, in each of which learned divines lecture, and students and pilgrims pursue researches into the spiritual arts of contemplation and mystical experience. There is also a very large library containing the volumes in Persian and Arabic written by the first pioneers and the subsequent leaders of the Sufic Way, and a valuable collection of other works on theology, ethics, philosophy and the high-road of the spirit. These are available for the use of both students and pilgrims under the guidance of the Murshed or Pir (i.e. the "guru" in Hindi), the spiritual director. On the other side of the shrine is the *Khaneqah*, or hospice, with rooms and equipment for the lodging and feeding of pilgrims. Here they may stay as long as they are able, without charge to themselves . . .

Abulfazl Hazeghi also summarises the teaching of the order, as given in a best-selling book written by the father of the present leader, which "makes clear for the ordinary man and woman how to practise this moral and spiritual discipline, and so to enjoy the fruits of the spirit in the daily life of this world."

Shaikh Sultanhussein's father wrote *Pand-i-Sāleh* ("Saleh's Advice") which has been reprinted in innumerable editions and become a household word amongst the religious in Iran. In it he describes the three steps a man must take to draw near to God:

1. SHARĪ'AT or "the Law" is the outward discipline of complete obedience to ethical and ritual requirements, in behaviour and worship;
2. TARĪQAT or "the Way" is the inner discipline of total obedience to the call of the spirit in the heart, calling for the abandonment of every high thing that exalts itself against the knowledge of God, the total subordination of the self, the elimination of self-will, the renunciation of every secondary interest and predilec-

tion, the dethroning of every idol and enthroning of the one
passion to know God and do His Will alone;

3. HAQĪQAT or "the Truth" is the entry into the spirit-filled service of
God which is perfect freedom, by which the soul comes to
know God and enjoy Him for ever . . .

*Sharī'at* is a discipline open to every man and woman, from the simplest
to the most erudite.

*Tarīqat* is a discipline open to all who have succeeded in bringing their
own lives into conformity with *Sharī'at*.

*Haqīqat* is given on earth only to such rare souls as make steps (1) and
(2) the only way of life they know or want to live.[6]

Squared design: *Ah-ḥamdu l-illāhi*: "Praise to God"
Turkish minaret, 16th century AD

# Journey to Reality

One Sufi "way" that is growing rapidly is the Yashruṭi order. It is named after a Shaikh who lived in the ancient port of Acca, Palestine, a hundred years ago. His great grandson became the leader in 1980. For many years the member of the Yashruṭi family with the greatest influence was a woman, Sayyida Fāṭima.

Today the order is spreading in many countries; in parts of Asia and Africa – Madagascar and Mozambique, for instance – as well as in Syria. Its appeal is widely heeded among Palestinians, a fact which reveals a little-known side of their character, and something of their spiritual roots.

The Yashruṭis form a branch of the Shādhili order, founded seven hundred years ago by a North African Shaikh, Abul-Hassan al-Shādhili, who died in AD 1258. It has a world-wide following and network.

It was in Kuala Lumpur that an expert on the history of the Shādhilis, Dr Abdul Majeed Mohamed Mackeen from Sri Lanka, gave the writer fresh insight into the ways of those who seek to follow the Sufi path. He and his brother talked of the experience that had come to them through their father. He played a record of a gathering of hundreds of people in Cairo, the sound capturing the rhythm of deepening concentration on the remembrance (*dhikr*) of God. A number of leading university men in Kuala Lumpur, he said, meet regularly for this same purpose of *dhikr*. He told me that I would learn more from Sayyida Fāṭima al-Yashruṭiyya, who lived in Beirut. There I visited her, and her sister and life-long companion, Miryam.

Sayyida Fāṭima was herself in her nineties. She was eight years old when her father, Shaikh Ali Nureddin al-Yashruṭi, died at the age of a hundred and eight, in the year 1891. He was born in 1783, and his life and hers between them span all the history of a fast-changing world since the French Revolution. Her brother Ibrahim, who succeeded his father as leader of the Yashruṭi branch of the order, was seventy years her senior, but they were very good friends. The early years of her life made the deepest impression on her. She had little or no formal education, but has written four books the last of which was finished in 1978, a few days before she died.[7]

*Journey to Reality* is the first of these. It is rich in the teachings, the songs, the prayers, of the order, but richer still in the scores of people one meets in its pages: men and women widely differing in character and circumstance, and all on the road to faith.

164

Acca, on the Palestinian coast, north of the modern city of Haifa, was in Ottoman days a busy port and military centre. There the Shaikh established himself in the 1850's. After his death in 1891, Sayyida Fāṭima lived there until the 1940's, when she left for Beirut.

In 1948 all the property of the order fell into the hands of the Israelis. She regarded this as unjust, but refused to harbour personal feelings of rancour about it. She said:

> I was resentful. I felt bitter for fifteen days. It took me as long as that to hand it all back to God. It is better not to be entangled with possessions.

There are many stages on the "journey to reality", and the study of them can take a lifetime. Something of the spirit of the men and women who through the centuries have led others to make that journey may be glimpsed through Sayyida Fāṭima and her books. As she says, "Mysticism is hard to explain. It is a wide sea. It is the relationship between man and God."

The life she so vividly remembers, in the home of her father and his followers, is described by her from the point of view of the women in his home – a rare source for such an account. The following pages are summarised from her book *Journey to Reality*, and from her conversation.

Asked about the strength of the Yashruṭi following today, Sayyida Fāṭima replied:

> Ours is a materialistic age, but there *are* those who follow the Way. Good men are always in the minority. But that does not matter. Numbers are not what counts.
>
> One person can be worth more than thousands. Many thousands are not worth one good man.

"In the Name of God, Most Gracious, Most Merciful"

# A Sufi Settlement in Acca

Shaikh Ali Nureddin al-Yashruṭi al-Hassani al-Husseini was born in Benzarta, Tunis, in the year AH 1208/AD 1783. He died in Acca, Palestine, in AH 1316/AD 1891.

He was a great shaikh and a very holy man. He was fortieth in spiritual descent from Shaikh Abul Hassan al-Shādhili, founder of the Shādhili order, and he inherited his spirit, even though there were thirty-nine shaikhs between them.

His father was a soldier. His mother, Miryam, was cultured in an age when few women had so much knowledge. She was the only daughter, and her father himself taught her to read and write. She married and had children, four of whom were growing up when suddenly, in one week, they all died of smallpox. Miryam, already middle-aged, was overcome with grief and despair. The family urged her husband to take another wife, so as to have children, but he loved his wife greatly and did not wish to do so. "Then God in His mercy put things right for her, and she bore a son – the great shaikh, my father. God took their grief away and gave them back happiness."

When this son grew up, he became a leader of the Shādhili order in Tunis. When the shaikh who had taught him died, he decided that the time had come to travel eastwards. After many adventures he reached Mecca, where he spent four years. He visited the tomb of his predecessor Al-Shādhili, near the Red Sea, then set his face to visit the holy city of Bait al-Maqdis (Jerusalem). He went by ship from Alexandria intending to land at Jaffa, but the ship was blown northwards along the coast. The passengers were put ashore at a point between Sidon and Beirut, where stands the tomb of the prophet Jonah.

The master of the ship refused to take any payment for carrying the Shaikh and his company. "I would like to reward you," said the Shaikh. and he explained to him his teaching and way of life. So this man was the first in that part of the world to enter into the life of the Sufi order through the Shaikh. He became one of his most faithful disciples.

The Shaikh settled outside Acca, and soon the crowds of those who came to learn from him grew to such proportions that it became necessary to build a centre (zāwiya, the word for any regular meeting place of a Sufi order). This was the first of many, in Acca, Jerusalem, Haifa, Damascus, Beirut, Rhodes and elsewhere.

The zāwiya in Acca was a big establishment. It was a centre of religion and learning, where everyone worked, and all took part in the common life. Strict attention was paid to health and hygiene. Food was provided for the disciples who came to visit the Shaikh, and there were at least four or five hundred a day. On special days the numbers would rise to one or two thousand.

Many men carried out what they learned from the Shaikh in their professions. Some gave up their worldly possessions and joined him. Most of these were from good families, or were scholars. One had been prominent in public life in Acca. He was put in charge of the practical side of running the *zāwiya* and performed this service perfectly.

An important general in the Ottoman army came to Acca. He had been stationed in Yemen, and was an alcoholic. One night he had had a dream, in which a man advised him to stop drinking. "You are my son," he said, "and you do not need to drink like this." A few nights later the dream was repeated. He asked the man in the dream who he was. "I am Ali Nureddin al-Yashruṭi," was the reply, "and I live in Acca. There is no man who is unable to repent and start to live a useful life."

Six months later, the general was transferred to Acca. He sought out Shaikh Ali Nureddin, took instruction from him, and came to live in a house near the *zāwiya*. As his faith increased, he brought many officers and soldiers under the Shaikh's influence. He lived in Acca for fifteen years, and gathered round him a group of army leaders who all worked in the service of the order.

The Shaikh loved birds and animals. No one could beat an animal in his presence, or put too heavy a load on it. One of the horses in the *zāwiya* lost its sight. The owner of an oil press wanted to buy it, so that it could turn the wheel, but the Shaikh forbade this. "The horse has gone blind in our service. It must have its food as long as it lives, as a reward for a life of toil."

## The Shaikh and His Family

My father had a great respect for women, both for their rights and for their duties, and he tried to raise the level of their education. When he married my mother she was illiterate. He brought in a special teacher to instruct her how to read and write, and himself gave her much encouragement, so that she reached a very high level of spiritual life.

Special lessons were given every morning to all the women in the house, not only those of his own family. He himself chose the books and the subjects, and appointed a lady teacher. Often he was with us himself. Everyone came, after which they went to their household tasks.

Young as I was, he began to teach me, explaining things so simply that I could understand. The other children in the house came to his lessons too. He taught me to treat all equally, whether rich or poor. Though he was a great shaikh and I was a little girl, he gave me an indelible picture of the Sufi way of life.

My father lived in exactly the same way as his disciples. He never smoked – he was not a man in the grip of habits. We were a household of sixty or seventy people, but the house was always quiet.

When I was five, he used to wake me to pray at night. My grandmother protested, but he said, "I want her to have the picture of me praying imprinted on her heart." He continued with his night prayers till the night before he died.

"In the Name of God, Most Gracious, Most Merciful"

# A Policeman's Faith

One of the key words in Sufi writings is "reality". The profound mysticism of Sufi saints and poets often inspires in their followers an attitude that is not in the western sense other-worldly, but which takes a very practical turn.

A genial policeman in Pune, India is an example, Shaikh Abdurrazak Shah Biyabani. His long years of service – for many of them as Deputy Superintendent – included those of his country's new independence, and he developed a strong sense of responsibility for the social life and needs of his fellow-countrymen.

After twenty-five years as a policeman he wrote a short book, *Glimpses of Reality*. It is a robust mixture of poetry and prose, dealing with the glories of Divine love, and the beauties of the rose, alongside the everyday needs of suffering humanity and the duty of responsible citizens to tackle them. He writes of "the reality with which we, as common men of action, are mostly concerned," comments a friend. He owes his personal convictions to a Sufi saint who died not many years ago, but he exhibits a certain impatience with religious experts, so-called "degree-holders" in the subject. The realisation of God must come to men through experience. The "higher understanding" must be brought within the reach of common man.

> It is of no use to try to root out corruption by fear of law that appeals only to the intellect. There should be a real appeal to the inner self, and actually a sort of hatred for corruption or other sins should be created in our hearts. In short the conscience should be enlivened This is actually an opportunity that has luckily come to the lot of public servants to serve God honestly and faithfully . . .
>
> People should be taught to think and think, and come to the right conclusion as to what is good and bad, and to consult their conscience as often as possible.
>
> A man who has never eaten or seen a mango will not get a correct idea of a mango, even if thousands of lectures are given to him about what a mango is. But when a man with a mango in his hand just shows it to him, he at once gets the idea, and when he eats it he will say, "Ah." Well, this is a sort of realisation. Only those who have realised God can lead you to the realisation of God, and not the learned philosophers who have no realisation.
>
> Nothing can be achieved without the purity of mind and heart . . . We must obey the dictates of our conscience through which our soul speaks out; and thus we will make ourselves impressionable to the voice of the Universal Soul.[8]

# The Building of a Sufi Meeting Place

The life and work of another Sufi, Shaikh Aḥmad al-'Alawi, has been vividly described in the book *A Sufi Saint of the Twentieth Century*, by Dr Martin Lings.[9] A doctor who attended the Shaikh observed the comings and goings of the hundreds who came to seek his inspiration, and describes how they worked together to make a worthy meeting place for him and his disciples.

The Shaikh died in 1934.

When I first met the Shaikh (in Mostaganem, Algeria) the present *zāwiyah* had not yet been built. A group of *fuqarā* (disciples) had bought the ground and made a present of it to the Shaikh, and the foundations had already been laid, but the troubles of 1914 interrupted the work, which was not resumed until 1920.

The way in which this *zāwiyah* was built is both eloquent and typical; there was neither architect – at least not in the ordinary sense – nor master-builder, and all the workmen were volunteers. The architect was the Shaikh himself – not that he ever drew up a plan or manipulated a set-square. He simply said what he wanted, and his conception was understood by the builders. They were by no means all from that part of the country. Many had come from Morocco, especially from the Riff, and some from Tunis, all without any kind of enlistment. The news had gone around that work on the *zāwiyah* could be started once more, and that was all that was needed. Among the Shaikh's North African disciples there began an exodus in relays; masons some, carpenters others, stone-cutters, workers on the roads, or even ordinary manual labourers, they knotted a few meagre provisions in a handkerchief and set out for the far-off town where the Master lived to put at his disposal the work of their hands. They received no wages. They were fed, that was all; and they camped out in tents. But every evening, an hour before the prayer, the Shaikh brought them together and gave them spiritual instruction. That was their reward.

They worked in this way for two months, sometimes three, and then went away once more, glad to have contributed to the work, and satisfied in spirit. Others took their place and after a certain time went off in their turn, to be immediately replaced by new arrivals, eager to start work. More always came, and there was never any lack of hands. This went on for two years, by the end of which the building was finished. This manifestation of simple and outspoken devotion gave me a deep sense of inward happiness. The world evidently still contained some individuals disinterested enough to put themselves, without any recompense, at the service of an ideal. Here, in the mid-twentieth century, was the same fervour that had built the cathedrals in the Middle Ages, and no doubt the actual building itself had taken place along somewhat similar lines. I was happy to have been an astonished eye-witness.

As soon as the *zāwiyah* was finished, the *fuqarā* said that they would like to have a big festival to celebrate its inauguration . . . [Disciples] came from all directions and all classes of society . . . I was specially struck by the most humble of them all, the Riff mountaineers, who had been travelling for a whole month, going on foot from hamlet to hamlet . . .

They had set out full of enthusiasm, like the pioneers of the gold-rush, but it was no temporal riches that they had come in search of. Their quest was purely spiritual, and they knew that they would not be deceived. I watched them motionless, silent . . . penetrated by the holiness of the place, with their chief aspirations realised. They were happy, in complete accord with themselves, in the Presence of God . . .

How had the Shaikh's fame spread so far? There was never any organised propaganda. The disciples made not the slightest attempt to proselytise. In any town or village that happened to contain some of their number, they had, and they still have today, their own little secluded *zāwiyahs*, each under the guidance of a *muqaddam*, that is one who is invested with the confidence and authority of the Shaikh. These little brotherhoods refrain on principle from all outward action, as if they were jealously bent on letting no one share their secrets. None the less, the influence spreads, and would-be novices are always coming forward to ask for initiation. They come from all walks of life.

One day I voiced my surprise to the Shaikh. He said:

"All those come here who feel troubled by the thought of God . . .

"They come to seek inward peace."

# Deliverance from Error

The great philosopher Abū Ḥāmid al-Ghazāli lived nine hundred years ago. His experience and his thinking still have great influence. The story of his conversion is often told. In AD 1095, at the height of his powers and his fame, he suddenly resigned from his professorship in Baghdad and went into retirement. Dissatisfied with the legalistic approach to religion, and the hair-splitting arguments of the scholastics, he set out to find the personal experience of God which alone would resolve his doubts and confusions.

He recounts the story himself in his book, *Deliverance from Error* (*al-munqidh min al-ḍalāl*), which ranks amongst the greatest works of religious literature:

> Then I turned my attention to the Way of the Sufis. I knew that it could not be traversed to the end without both doctrine and practice, and that the gist of the doctrine lies in overcoming the appetites of the flesh and getting rid of its evil dispositions and vile qualities, so that the heart may be cleared of all but God; and the means of clearing it is *dhikr Allāh*, i.e. commemoration of God and concentration of every thought upon Him. Now, the doctrine was easier to me than the practice, so I began by learning their doctrine from the books and sayings of the Shaykhs, until I acquired as much of their Way as it is possible to acquire by learning and hearing, and saw plainly that what is most peculiar to them cannot be learned, but can only be reached by immediate experience and ecstasy and inward transformation . . .
>
> I became convinced that I had now acquired all the knowledge of Sufism that could possibly be obtained by means of study; as for the rest, there was no way of coming to it except by leading the mystical life. I looked on myself as I then was. Worldly interests encompassed me on every side. Even my work as a teacher – the best thing I was engaged in – seemed unimportant and useless in view of the life hereafter. When I considered the intention of my teaching, I perceived that instead of doing it for God's sake alone I had no motive but the desire for glory and reputation. I realised that I stood on the edge of a precipice and would fall into Hell-fire unless I set about to mend my ways . . . Conscious of my helplessness and having surrendered my will entirely, I took refuge with God as a man in sore trouble who has no resource left. God answered my prayer and made it easy for me to turn my back on reputation and wealth and wife and children and friends.[10]

# The Nature of Man

"To tame the animal in man is the task of religion: to effect a balance between what we are and what we should be." The possibility of a profound change in human character was part of Al-Ghazāli's concept of life. Dr Ali Issa Othman explains this:

By the very attribute which offers to man a higher potential than the rest of creatures, man is capable of becoming peculiarly wicked and, in the attainment of his worldly ends, may exhibit the qualities of animals and the devil . . .

Under the skin of every individual, therefore, there are – in Al-Ghazāli's phraseology – the qualities of a "pig (appetite), a dog (anger), a devil (both) or a sage." The individual is similar to a pig when he is untrustworthy, extravagant, niggardly or hypocritical; similar to a dog when he is reckless, haughty, self-admiring and disdainful. He is capable of combining all the bad qualities of animals and becoming the devil himself. In such an extreme his qualities are deceit, stratagem, trickery, audacity, and love for agitation and fraud.

But the "sage" in man, disposed to knowledge and wisdom, may through religious guidance expose the wiles of the "devil" in him and keep the "pig" and the "dog" in subjection. The wrath of man is turned to gratitude.

The establishment of a genuine feeling of humility, as a result of his knowledge of his dependency upon the bounties of God's love . . . enables the individual to turn . . . to wisdom . . . Under such a state of being, the pig in man turns to chastity, patience, temperance, gentleness and reverence, and the dog turns to courage, generosity, clemency and true dignity.[11]

## God's Light

All worship is rooted in the Qur'ān. One of its most famous verses, on which much devotion has been based, comes in the *Sūrat-al-nūr*, the Chapter of Light:

> In the Name of God, Most Gracious, Most Merciful
>
> God is the Light
> Of the heavens and the earth.
>
> The parable of His Light
> Is as if there were a Niche
> And within it a Lamp:
> The Lamp enclosed in Glass:
> The glass as it were
> A brilliant star:
> Lit from a blessed Tree,
> An Olive, neither of the East
> Nor of the West,
> Whose oil is well-nigh
> Luminous,
> Though fire scarce touched it:
>
> Light upon Light!
> God doth guide
> Whom He will
> To His Light:
> God doth set forth Parables
> For men: and God
> Doth know all things.[12]

# PART SIX
## *The Road Ahead*

# CHAPTER SEVENTEEN

# *Future Imperative*

There is a Divine imperative by which the struggle in the created world between right and wrong, good and evil, is unrelenting until God gives the verdict.

Mohammed Abduh[1]

We should think about our future in multi-generational terms.

Ziauddin Sardar[2]

The future of Muslims in the modern world cannot be considered in isolation. We have first to consider the future of man... The secular civilisation of the West is facing a grave crisis... It is against this perspective that one should consider the problem of Muslims in the world today.

Altaf Gauhar[3]

We have a mission today in comparison with which the mighty events of the past such as the European Renaissance or the French and Soviet Revolutions must fade into insignificance... nothing less than to give a fresh lease of life to dying humanity.

Sayyid Abul Hasan Ali Nadwi[4]

The future faced by the Muslim fifth of mankind is no different from that common to the rest. The spectres of hunger and of nuclear destruction, of inflation and war, know no boundaries, nor do the dreams of universal justice and plenty.

Across the Muslim world there are as many varied voices to be heard as elsewhere: reasoned hopes and desperate fears, despair and optimism, cynicism and idealism, ideas that are world-embracing or egocentric. Some experience the power and problems of unaccustomed wealth. Most struggle for a living. Many are absorbed in the difficulties of adapting to an industrialised society. There are internal stresses between old and young, and deep resentments of pressures on family life attributed to an alien and materialistic West.

Islam's inner capacity for renewal has more than once surprised both friend and foe. The initial conquests swiftly led to the fostering of a great civilisation. When in turn other conquerors invaded Muslim lands, Islam found the power to win them to her fold. It has at various times raised up reformers to rekindle the light of faith when it had grown dim. It has as good a chance as any other faith or ideology – Muslims would say a better one – of holding and extending its power over the hearts and wills of men.

But what is at stake today is the future of the human race itself, not of this or that religion. This larger question is what concerns forward-looking Muslims.

Many of the best minds devoted to the questions of the environment, the feeding of mankind, the conquest of disease, the bridging of the gap between rich and poor, are inspired by the faith and tenets of Islam. Others explore the role of faith at a time when, at an apparent peak of scientific power, man is threatened by a failure of nerve, by the loss of the will to find and implement solutions to the questions that face him. As crisis follows crisis, panic tends to paralyse thought and hinder far-sighted action. In such a situation faith emerges in a role which many have denied it: as a liberating force giving an inner security valuable to the free play of thought and initiative. Men and women who act in a larger perspective, instead of reacting to every storm that blows, are an essential element in every scheme for betterment, every hope of reconciliation.

That Islam can contribute such men and women to the common need is not the least of gifts to the world community. Some have already spoken in these pages. A few more voices may be added, on what they see as their mission today.

# Islam has a World Mission

*Islam's Mission Is a World Mission* is the title of one of a series of books published by the Higher Council for Islamic Affairs, Cairo. The author, Dr Ali Abdul Halim Mahmud, explores the universal character of Islam's message, which is as urgently needed now as it was in the world situation contemporary with the Prophet.

The search for the way of life and thought that is fundamentally right for mankind leads, he says, to Islam in its deepest sense, of submission to God and the laws of His creation. "Religion with God is Islam," he quotes: and all sincere beliefs and obedience to God wherever they are found are in their essence Islam.

God's message to man as to how to live, and how to manage the earth, has often been neglected and debased. Preached by many prophets at many times to different peoples, and sealed by the mission of the final Prophet Muḥammad, this way of thinking and living demands the cleansing away of all false elements and the humility to be led along the road of progress in the service of God. It is not a question of which of God's prophets is right, but of seeking the straight and open road of God's teaching.

The book also explores the type of character produced by this yielding to God. To a sick humanity, Islam can offer a cure that matches each disease, a solution that fits each problem: but this is true in no superficial sense. It is in the area of motivation and purpose that the change must be sought: in a purity of intention only God can give. The first Muslims were victorious because they saw their warfare in the light of the struggle between good and evil, truth and falsehood: the fight to free men from servitude to men, for service to God. It is this battle that the men of God must fight today:

> The religion that the Prophet brought was directed towards mankind as a whole. Islam based its system on the concept that all men form one community (*umma*) without distinction of race or colour, language or culture, history or religion.
>
> The spread of Islam acted like sap in a leafless tree. It came into a world of social and religious confusion.
>
> Then as now, the perplexities were the same. They arose in questions of relationships: what is the relation between God and man? between man and his fellow man? between man and those who govern him? There were civilisations in being in both west and east but they had failed to solve these questions. Islam therefore came into a world

thirsting for health and security, and for a civilised order that would provide these things.

The morals of Islam worked on human nature in the same way that fire purifies iron, and melts it so that it can be forged into an effective instrument. Men cast in this mould transcend the borders of race. The same moral qualities were passed on by the first Muslims to those who followed them.

Islam is not a novel religion that appeared in Arabia fourteen centuries ago, preached by the Prophet Muḥammad. It is the religion God made known on the day when man first appeared on earth. He taught those first men the one sound way of living for all the human species. The prophets He later sent at intervals to different places came with the same summons: to submit to God; and this call, given by all the Prophets, was crowned by the mission of Muḥammad.

The Qur'ānic verse, "Religion with God is Islam", embraces all the sects founded by the different prophets. It breathes a universal spirit and includes many methods and obligations. A true Muslim, according to the Qur'ān, must be clear of any taint of false regard for other than the God he serves. He must be pure in both his beliefs and his actions. This applies, whatever sect, time or place he may represent. Religion that does not have this true character of Islam has been misused by men as a bond of nationalism, or a tool of fanaticism, or even a means of worldly prosperity. Such false religion only adds to corruption. That is why the Qur'ān says that those who do not follow Islam in its purity are permanently at a loss.

In general, the religion of Islam has two aims. First, to free the mind and spirit from involvements, the invisible bonds that hold them in subjection to material things: and to save people from a humiliating servitude to others who are no better than themselves.

Second, to provide the right goal for all man's actions, and give him a purity of motive towards God and his fellow men.

These are the twin sources of the Islamic spirit. At this present time they are a pointer to the universality of religion and its world-wide character since "There is no religion apart from Islam."[5]

# Muslim Unity in the Contemporary World

"A compelling and unrealised dream," says Dr Inamullah Khan, Secretary General of the World Muslim Conference, speaking of the Muslim ideal of an all-embracing world community rising above clime and country, race and colour. In many Western capitals, recent buildings of great beauty give expression to this vision. At the same time organisations have been established with the aim of making the ideal into a reality.

The Muslim World League (*Rābitat al-'ālam al-islāmī*), formed in Mecca in 1962, aims to convey the message of Islam throughout the world in many ways, for instance by making the best use of the annual pilgrimage and by raising the level of Islamic publications. It has published translations of the Holy Qur'ān in many languages, including Hausa, Japanese, Chinese, and English. In 1965 it sponsored the authoritative translation and commentary by Abdullah Yusuf Ali. The League has observer status at the United Nations as also has the World Muslim Conference.[6]

The Organisation of the Islamic Conference (OIC), established in 1971, organises periodic meetings of heads of Islamic states or their foreign ministers. It has a permanent secretariat in Jeddah. Its first Secretary General was the former premier of Malaysia, Tunku Abdul Rahman. The *World Muslim Gazetteer* (1985) lists 46 member states, 19 organisations operating under its auspices (including the Islamic Development Bank and others in the fields of economics, science, law and culture): and 20 associate members and observers, such as the Arab League, the Islamic Council of Europe, the Muslim World League and the World Muslim Conference.[7]

The World Muslim Conference (*Mo'tamar al-'ālam al-islāmī*) had its origin in a meeting called by King Abdul-Aziz Ibn Saud in Mecca in 1926. Its headquarters are in Karachi. Dr Inamullah Khan, its Secretary-General for many years, gives the ideal of the Muslim community a spiritual rather than a political emphasis. In an article in 1975, as preparations were being made for the celebration of a new century of Islam, he analysed the current situation, under the title, *Islam in the Contemporary World*.[8] He rejects four categories of thinkers: the "no-changers", the westernisers, the apologists, and the backward-looking revivalists. He himself aims to re-express Islam in modern terms.

When we look back at our history, we of the contemporary world see not only the bright side but also the dark side; we see where our weakness and where our strength lay. The fact is that we were given the basic principles of a grand ideology which we had to implement, but we, as human beings, erred on many occasions in this great but difficult task, and it is now our endeavour to realise and rectify the errors that were made in the past.

Islam does not need to be modernised. Islam has always been modern . . . With its emphasis on reason and tolerance, [it] is today as capable of making its contribution to the advancement of man as it was in the early centuries. With its emphasis on knowledge, [it] is fully capable of meeting the needs of modern society. Islam will therefore continue to be a civilising force.

Looking deep beneath the surface, we can see that it is the Demon of Materialism that is playing havoc . . . Both the contending world blocs of today are worshippers of materialism . . . To quote the great reformer Jamaluddin Afghani, "The struggle in the world today is basically one between Religion and Materialism," and we followers of Islam will welcome every joint effort by the believers in God and spiritual values, of whatever religion, to stem the tide of atheism, materialism and the denial of spiritual values which is threatening the peace and well-being of humanity.[9]

# The Encounter of Man and Nature

Centuries ago Muslim scientists gave to Europe the knowledge on which Western scientific development was built. The story is many-sided. The "Arabic" numerals which freed arithmetic from the laboured and limited calculations of the Roman system are only one example of the debt. In mathematics and chemistry, navigation and pharmacy, astronomy and medicine, Arab scientists passed on the body of knowledge, and the tools for experiment, which the scholars of the Renaissance were to develop.

Now in their turn the peoples of the Muslim world are learning from the West the technical skills by which in modern times nature has so largely been subdued. In their efforts to avoid the disruptions which have accompanied the application of these discoveries, they may yet give back to the West a further gift: the wholeness of life and unity of outlook which has largely been lost in the fragmentation of Western thought and living, though it is intrinsically as much a part of the Christian as of the Muslim world view.

One of the Muslim thinkers who have explored this line of enquiry is Dr Seyyed Hossein Nasr. He combines the disciplines of science and mysticism in a way that was common in an earlier age, but is rare now that knowledge has been to such a degree compartmentalised. With the background of a Harvard doctorate in the History of Science he turned his attention to the scientific traditions of the East, and their relevance to the questions that confront man today.

He sees the key in man's encounter with nature. Behind the endemic crises lie causes deep in the history and attitudes of the scientific revolution of the West. Man has become the plunderer of his natural environment, instead of its viceroy: he takes out of it whatever he wants, instead of caring for it as the representative and steward of a higher Power.

Unless this fundamental relationship is put right, there is no hope of peace and little prospect of survival, says Dr Nasr. The destruction of the equilibrium between man and nature underlies the dangers of war, of overpopulation and pollution. Few are willing to look reality in the face and accept the fact that there is no peace possible in human society as long as the attitude towards nature and the whole natural environment is one based on aggression and war. In order to gain this peace with nature there must be peace with the spiritual order, and respect for the immutable supra-human realities which are the source of all human values.

The believing Muslim is quite clear that modern knowledge does not threaten faith in God. Rather, every new discovery reveals more of the wonder of God's creation. There are verses in the Qur'ān which can be interpreted as foreshadowing later scientific discoveries. What is far more important, it blesses and commands the use and growth of knowledge. The laboratory worker with the Qur'ān propped up above his sophisticated pharmaceutical machinery knows this, and so does the medical teacher in Al-Azhar who maintains that scientists, to be effective, must hold fast to the standards and integrity that faith gives. Such men look back to the fact that Islamic civilisation was the torchbearer of scientific knowledge for centuries.

To meet the spiritual crisis of modern man, however, will take a deeper travail, "in the hope of finding once again a sacred foundation for science itself."[10] To do this calls for an interplay on a level far removed from the quick reactions and hurtful thrusts of controversy. It demands a radical change in thought patterns, assumptions that have their roots deep in the history of the past. This applies especially to assumptions in the scientific field, which in the West have allowed a scientific revolution to develop outside the range of Christian thought. The attitude to nature of St Francis of Assisi in his Song of Creation, with its "startling reminder of the possibility of a reverential attitude towards nature . . . outside all human utility"[11], was lost by some later religious thinkers, who put aside the question of nature and considered man's salvation with total disregard of the rest of God's creation. The Muslim mind has always lived at the level of wonder vis-à-vis the world of nature.[12] But Western science developed "totally divorced from the one experiment that was central for the men of old, namely experiment with oneself through a spiritual discipline."[13]

> In the old days man had to be saved from nature. Today nature has to be saved from man in both peace and war. Many labour under the illusion that only war is evil and that if only it could be averted man could go on peacefully to create paradise on earth. What is forgotten is that . . . man is waging an incessant war upon nature. The official state of war is no more than an occasional outburst of an activity that goes on all the time within the souls of men . . . Whether one pollutes water resources in a single bombing or does so over a twenty year period is essentially the same: the only difference is a matter of time.

> Perhaps the answer to the burning question of how to avoid war . . .

lies in coming to peace with nature ... in harmony and equilibrium with Heaven, and ultimately with the Source and Origin of all things.[14]

It is interesting to note how the cry of a few seers in the wilderness just a generation ago has today become the battle-cry of so many.

Today a great many people realise that the goal of the "conquest of nature", which has seemed the most obvious aim of modern civilisation, can no longer be pursued ... All the problems caused by the unilateral attitude of modern man towards nature, from over-population and mass pollution to the lowering of the quality of human life itself and the threat of its actual destruction, have at least caused those capable of reflection to pause a moment and examine the assumptions upon which modern science and its applications are based ... Nature shorn of all spiritual and metaphysical considerations ... leaves aside a whole aspect of its reality.

The realisation by modern ecologists that one must study the whole environment as a complex unity in which everything is interrelated can only be complete if it also embraces the psychological and spiritual levels of reality and hence ultimately the Source of all that is.[15]

Egyptian thorn, from a list of medicinal plants, Iraq, late 14th century AD

# Environment and Resources

The care of the environment and the handling of world resources are world priorities. The Qur'ān's injunctions on stewardship of property, as well as its stress on mutual responsibility, are a source of inspiration to Muslims at work in these fields.

In this light may be seen the initiative from Algeria which first suggested the holding of a World Food Conference. This took place in Rome in November 1974. Its Secretary-General was Sayed Ahmed Marei, Special Assistant to President Sadat and formerly Managing Director of the Agricultural Agency which carried through the Egyptian Land Reforms in the 1950's. As "an unrepentant optimist" he spoke of the capacity of the world community to deal with the world food problem, if the will could be generated for an equitable sharing of mankind's accumulated wealth and experience.

One hopeful possibility that emerged at the World Food Conference was that of a large increase in agricultural production in the Sudan. Discussing this, Sayyed Mohamed Ahmed Mahgoub says:

> The coming generation should anchor the country's economic policy on a very interesting and relevant aspect of their religion. The practice of private ownership in Islam, where the owner is seen as an agent acting for the whole community, still holds its own compared with prevalent conceptions of ownership in capitalist countries. And it is certainly preferable to the Communist system of collective ownership. Islam has laid down a set of rules for the conduct of ownership, trade and taxation which conform with the activities of a modern state.[16]

The objectives of the Islamic economic order, says Muhammad Umar Chapra, Economic Adviser to the Saudi Monetary Agency, are universal: freedom, equity, economic well-being for all, and a synthesis of the material and the spiritual which does not neglect the spiritual needs of the human personality.[17]

The extent of the changes involved in applying such principles is apparent in the words of a leading figure in the World Environment Programme.

Dr Mostafa Tolba was formerly President of the Egyptian Academy of Scientific Research and Technology. When the United Nations Environment programme was established in 1973 he became its Deputy Director, and later its Director. In an interview in April 1974 he stated:

> In the long term – and even in the short term, here and now – we

will have to adopt a new life-style. We have to think in terms of the management of the environment as a whole, of eco-development.

If we are going to accept this idea, it will definitely mean that we shall have to look into our social habits and all we are doing to our environment, and try to think what should be done to make it better. There will need to be some changes – and some of these may be radical.

I do not think this is the responsibility of the developed countries alone. We have to deal with the aspirations of the peoples in the developing countries, and some of these desires might lead to a level of wastefulness in certain areas, comparable to that which has characterised the use of products in the developed countries.

The developing countries *must* develop. Most of the environmental problems in these countries are caused by under-development. But it is also a must that they should find the right goal. They should not take on the same short-sighted aims that have brought us into the present dilemma. We have to benefit from what the developed world has been through. We can learn from their errors and mistakes, and can find a better basis on which to build.

The philosophy of greed and waste that has been propagated from the developed world is something that cannot be allowed any longer. For the future, the question must be of *need*, rather than greed.

Is it to be what we want? Or what we need? This is a strong moral point. Will we come to the point of deciding what we need? And are we strong enough to force ourselves to stop there, rather than taking what we want? Because there is no end to what we want. We have a fixed amount of resources, a growing population, and growing aspirations all over the world. So here is the point. We have to resist the temptations of what we want.

Either we take this responsibility on ourselves, and act on it – or we will be faced with catastrophe. Such a catastrophe could take the form of a hundred million people dying of hunger. That figure is an immediate threat, if there should be drought in two or three areas in the world. We do not need to let one hundred million people die, in order to realise that there is a problem to solve.[18]

# A Contract with the Future

Can the future differ from the past? The Qur'ān points to this possibility for both individuals and nations. Both can change course and turn from evil to good.

The Qur'ānic verses on repentance (*tauba*) are gathered together by Altaf Gauhar in his book, *Translations from the Qur'ān*. "The ability to repent is the distinguishing quality of the believer," he comments. "Repentance is not merely the negation of the past; it is essentially a contract with the future."

The Quranic conception of repentance is an intimate personal act. It reflects a moment of decision when one makes up one's mind to break with a course of action and simultaneously adopt another course.

This process of repentance and forgiveness started with Adam.

When a person repents he does not explain his conduct. He says, "Admittedly I have committed wrong but given an opportunity I shall make amends." In this sense repentance means asking for an opportunity to prove oneself. And this is how it becomes a contract for the future.

Remission and hope of forgiveness alone can extricate a man from the vicious circle of sin. Once he loses hope, he turns into a veritable devil.

Nations, like individuals, commit themselves to pursuits which result in their destruction. They too are given warnings and offered opportunities to reform themselves . . . A nation, when it is misguided by its affluence and power and adopts oppressive ways, is bound to come a cropper. But even as it is hurrying to a dismal end, should it realize its mistake and abandon the path of defiance, reverting humbly to God, it will find its situation dramatically altered.

The view that the consequences of sin are unavoidable and man must suffer the punishment for his lapses is rejected by the Qur'ān. Such a view is misleading as it excludes all possibility of improvement.

A believer enters into a contract with God with full sense of responsibility, pledging his life and property to His cause. But there are moments when he tends to treat his life and property as his own, forgetting that God is the real master. These moments occur quite often . . . It is the willingness to revert to God again and again . . . which distinguishes a believer and invests his faith with permanence . . . A believer is one who returns readily to the right course after being led astray.[19]

# The Health of Nations

"God will not change the condition of a people until
they change what is in their hearts."[20]

This famous verse in the Qur'ān is frequently cited today in discussion on the state of the world and its future. Deep in Muslim
thinking is the conviction that progress depends on the straightness of
a man's character and the quality of his response to the will and
purpose of God.

However complex the situation, the interaction of God's goodness
and man's sincerity brings hope.

Al-Ghazāli once spoke of good men as both the salt of society and
what holds it together. Today a voice from Africa brings a closing
comment on this theme. The Muslims of Eritrea have a long and
troubled history, dating from the time of the Prophet himself. Shaikh
Mohammed Ahmad Surur writes:

God has His ways with His creation. If nations are to live, they must
have among them a group of people who raise the challenge of right
and wrong. Such a group varies at different times, but in every century
we find people who dedicate their lives to guiding their fellow men.
Where no such group is found, the people perish and chaos and corruption spread.

Those who put right what is wrong save nations from destruction.
They are doctors of men. A sick man who does not find a doctor, or
does not take his advice, will die. This is the relationship between
nations and those who set out to change them.

Nobility of personality, springing from high morals – men with this
type of character are the new factor strong enough to spread the spirit
of peace and tolerance. They bring a new orientation towards ending
tyranny, removing bitterness from men's hearts and stopping the mad
rush towards materialism.

As for me, I pray Almighty God that I shall see the day when ordinary
men, responsible leaders, and indeed every world statesman, work
together to put an end to selfishness. Then by God's grace our world
will be set free from its present bitterness and fear.

And God is able to accomplish this.[21]

# Supplement I

## Memorandum by Abdel Khalek Hassouna

Much of the material in this book results from replies to questions put forward in the perspective of the need for common action by men of faith in the modern world. In asking these questions I made it clear that my purpose was not to write about Islam, but to offer a platform for Muslims to give their best thought and experience.

Abdel Khalek Hassouna, Secretary General of the Arab League from 1952 to 1971, was among those who welcomed this approach. When I first met him in Beirut in 1968, he was presiding over an Arab League conference. He asked if he could reply in writing and at leisure to my questions. Much of what he wrote has been absorbed into the rest of the book, but certain questions are answered in this memorandum, so as to give a fuller insight into the mind of one Arab elder statesman.

Hassouna's career and the application of his principles have already been illustrated in the story of the Lebanon crisis of 1958.[1] A life such as his, in the midst of the diplomatic vicissitudes of the past fifty years in the Middle East, has had its successes and its failures. Through them all he has kept faith with the principles he learned as a boy. The riches of the Qur'ān and of the life of the Prophet have been a living part of his search for contemporary solutions.

The combination he enjoyed – a boyhood education in the Qur'ān and a Cambridge degree in Law – is not uncommon, whatever form the western qualification may take, be it a science doctorate or a course at the Harvard School of Business Administration. It is minds with this double training that from the Arab side negotiate the political and economic developments of the day:

Question: What is the basis of unity in the Muslim World?
Answer: Three points may be given in reply to this question.
1. The belief is cultivated by Islam that all people, not only Muslims, are of one origin, namely Adam. This obviates differences of sex, colour, blood, language or nationality.
2. Each Muslim feels himself a member of one Islamic nation, and this contributes to the promotion of co-operation and joint efforts. This feeling is manifest in one of the Prophet's traditional sayings, "The

faithful are like the members of the body: if one of them complains all the others feel restless and feverish."

3. Islam is opposed to any exaggerated boasting about one's homeland, race or tribe. It teaches Muslims that the whole earth is the homeland of man and that all people are the sons of God; hence one's boasting should be of one's devotion to God, the God of all people. This was expressed by a poet who said, "While others boast of being the sons of Kais or Tamim, my only father is Islam. I have no other father." The Qur'ān clarifies this by saying, "If your fathers and your sons, your brethren and your wives, your tribe and the wealth you have acquired . . . are dearer to you than Allah and His messenger and striving in His way: then wait till Allah bringeth His command to pass. Allah guideth not wrong-doing folk."[2]

In other words, true Islam emancipates Muslims from the limitations of fanaticism, bias and personal interest. It integrates them all into the general concept of Islam, namely absolute obedience to God and to His prophet. The resulting unity in the Islamic world should serve as a natural basis for intellectual unity, and pave the way for unity between civilisations.

Question: How can the Muslim World contribute to the future of civilisation?

Answer: For over a thousand years Islamic civilisation was the highest in the world.

When Arab Muslims communicated their principles and ideals from the Arab peninsula – the cradle of Islam – to all parts of the inhabited world at that time, they were well received by the Persians, Romans, Indians, Egyptians and others, all of whom had developed a high level of material civilisation. These profited from the principles of justice, equality, fraternity, tolerance and mercy propagated by Islam, as well as by its quest for knowledge and its encouragement of useful work. Arab Muslims, on the other hand, copied certain branches of knowledge from the countries they conquered with the aim of spreading the new religion.

The material civilisation of these countries was much superior to that of the Arabs. Mixing this material civilisation with their spiritual one, the Arabs made use of the combination to administer and develop their state. The Khalifs encouraged the translation into Arabic of books connected with different cultures, sciences and arts, and placed them at the disposal of scholars.

The Arabs and Muslims also made their own contribution by

developing these sciences and arts. They introduced numerous important additions without which, historians admit, there would have been a wider gap separating ancient and modern civilisation.

Muslims offered their civilisation and culture to the whole world. Islamic universities in both East and West, particularly the universities of Spain, were frequented by students and lovers of culture who came to quench their thirst for knowledge. What they took back to their own countries served as a beacon of science and culture, and led on to the age of the Renaissance.

When the period of decline overtook the Islamic world, the seeds of Islamic civilisation had already been transplanted in Europe. They began to yield their fruit in the domains of medicine, astronomy, mathematics, physics, chemistry, anatomy, engineering, industry, social science, music, philosophy, pharmacy. Through advance in these fields, Europeans acquired the means to gain power and supremacy over others. This was particularly due to their acquaintance with the experimental aspects of science, in which, according to historians of science, the Arabs were pioneers.

It is perhaps unfair to attribute present-day civilisation to the West alone. Actually, it is a universal civilisation, the foundations of which were laid by all the peoples who had developed previous civilisations. The gist of it was conveyed to Europe through the medium of Islamic civilisation.

These facts help to provide an answer to the question: how can the Islamic world contribute to the future of civilisation? The Islamic world did actually contribute to the development of a world civilisation which prevailed for at least one thousand years and which offered itself as a nucleus for present-day civilisation. The latter, however, has adopted a local and materialistic character, claiming to be a separate entity unrelated to the civilisations which preceded it. Its pride has been intensified because science and technology have subjugated for it huge natural forces which have enabled it to exercise new forms of control on earth, and to seek the conquest of space. If this civilisation is to recapture the elements which characterised the Islamic era, it will have to aim at the establishment of peace based on justice. It must renounce colonialism, usurpation, exploitation, racial discrimination, class strife, materialism and the supremacy of the machine. All these contradict the real spirit of Christianity and the humane teachings of Christ.

The first contribution the Islamic world made to building a civilised world lay in its humane beliefs, concepts and moral values.

The second contribution is found today in the way Islamic people cherish and respect the United Nations and its agencies, as well as the Universal Declaration of Human Rights.

The third contribution is the policy of positive neutrality, and non-alignment with either of the two conflicting blocs dividing the world at present. The adoption of such a policy reflects a desire to maintain peace and to safeguard civilisation from the destruction of war in this nuclear age.

Contemporary thinkers and scientists in the Islamic world are meanwhile trying to renew their own civilisation and help it resume its role in the promotion of universal civilised values. To achieve this end, they are trying to express the civilisation of their peoples in modern terms.

The Islamic world occupies a central geographical position. This helps it to play a role in bringing other doctrines and civilisations closer to each other and paving the way for compromises capable of convincing all because they contain the best of each.

Question:  What has Islam to say to the scientist who is an atheist?
Answer:    Islam has many arguments against the atheism often proclaimed in the name of science. In propagating its message, Islam appeals to the intellect and seeks the help of scientific arguments and logic.

Science according to the Qur'ān is comprehensive, and based on reason. It is essentially an intellectual judgment applied to both material creatures and moral concepts. Without moral concepts there can be no knowledge of material particles or physical laws, mathematical or arithmetical proportions.

The first order in the Qur'ān was an order to read, and hence to acquire knowledge. Religion and science are one in Islam, because religion constitutes knowledge of both the spiritual and the material world. The Prophet Muḥammad was ordered in the Qur'ān to pray for further knowledge. The Qur'ān made the men of learning witnesses along with Allah and His angels for the greatest of facts, namely the Oneness of God. "Allah (Himself) is witness that there is no God save Him. And the angels and the men of learning (too are witnesses)."[3]

In seeking to prove the existence of God and to reaffirm the monotheistic belief, the Qur'ān made the miracles of nature the means of realising God's existence and greatness. Just as scientists deduce physical laws from their experiments, the Qur'ān rendered the whole universe a laboratory for intellectual experiments designed to prove the existence of God.

God is One because the process of creation shows the mark of a single craftsman and because natural laws do not come into clash or contradiction. The denial of God's existence needs more proofs and evidence than the affirmation of His existence. It is impossible to think that nature, the source of all wisdom and knowledge, is as it is without a cause and without a Creator who is administering it, controlling its stars and harmonising its laws.

Scientifically-minded people have rejected some religions because they spoke of God in terms of superstitious pictures which are unacceptable to the mind. The picture of God in the Qur'ān, however, is a purely rational one derived from His acts in the universe and in the soul, and it is only through this rational picture that His existence and perfection can be ascertained.

Some people have been misled by vanity and illusion into the belief that they have become gods in this age and that they have to depend entirely on themselves and leave nothing to God. Such people seem to have forgotten that man did not create himself, that he has no choice in either his birth or death, that he cannot escape from God and that he is entirely unable to manufacture anything identical with the human mind, that wonderful God-made machine which is working out the scientific miracles of which man boasts. The key to sound thinking is to admit that man cannot escape judgment.

Even if man arrives at the secret of making everything, he will always be called upon to answer the eternal question: Who created me? Who am I? How huge this universe is! Who created it? And for what end?

Question:  Islam enjoins fighting a Holy War. It also promises peace. The *Jihād* in a modern setting – what is it fought for? What is it fought against?

Answer:  Islam means struggling to ensure freedom of worship, prevent religious dissension, and secure the life of humble folk through the fulfilment of God's commands. It seeks to communicate the Islamic call to all people, who are free to take it or leave it.

What Islam is fighting against is the use of force to impose religion, the sowing of dissension, and any attack on humble folk or infringement of their rights.

This is expressed in many verses of the Qur'ān. "Sanction is given unto those who fight because they have been wronged."[4] "Fight in the way of Allah against those who fight against you, but begin not hostilities."[5] "And one who attacketh you, attack him in like manner as he attacked you."[6] "And fight them until persecution is no more, and religion is for Allah. But if they desist, then let there be no hostility except against wrong-doers."[7] It is evident from these verses that Islam permits fighting only for defending freedom of worship, and ensuring that God's call be communicated to all people without any attempt to impose it on them.

This means that Islam was not imposed by the sword as its enemies claim. People were converted to Islam by their own choice because the life it promised them was better than their previous life. Muslims invaded other countries to ensure that the Call would reach the masses everywhere. Those who chose to adhere to their previous creeds were not in any way forced to become Muslims and up till the present day religious minorities in Islamic countries enjoy freedom of worship. They practise their rights under the protection of Islam, which threatens to punish anyone who harms the "People of the Scriptures" or those who have a covenant with Muslims. Had not Islam protected the freedom of worship, these minorities would not have remained in Islamic countries until now.

Islam spread to China, Malaysia, Indonesia and the Philippines without fighting. It similarly spread in many African countries through conviction alone.

Question:  How did Muḥammad deal with the divisions in Arabia?
Answer:  Muḥammad is the example of the ideal of the "complete man". His personality is an enchanting study, even from the human aspect: his simplicity, depth, modesty, love of humanity and tolerance. He truly represents the virtues Allah has willed to be the attributes of man. The Qur'ān refers to him in the following verses: "Lo! thou art of a tremendous nature."[8] "The Grace of Allah toward thee hath been infinite."[9] He was a model to be followed as a child, a man, a husband, a father, a son, a trader, a leader, a prophet, a teacher, a legislator, a friend, a statesman and a loving and generous companion.

The Arabs were divided into clans and tribes, fighting each other for the slightest reason. Muḥammad dealt with this situation by instilling into their mind and heart the divine call. This call informed them that Allah created men grouped in peoples and tribes to get acquainted with each other and not to oppose and fight each other, and that all of them were brothers by origin and faith.

The Prophet showed the Arabs that vengeance, feuds and hatred belong to the atheist rather than to the believer, and must be wiped out of their hearts. No doubt the Prophet's compassion and open-mindedness were tools used by Allah to unify the divided Arabs, but the Qur'ān attributes the miracle of unity to Allah alone. He it was who wiped out of their hearts the prejudices of the Days of Ignorance (the *Jāhilīya*, before the Prophet came) as well as the pride they took in their fathers and forefathers. Allah urged them to be modest and not to boast to one another, thus establishing mutual respect among them.

Question: Do you think that all the "People of the Book" (Jews and Christians as well as Muslims) have a common responsibility for the rest of the world?

Answer: I certainly do. The Qur'ān tells the followers of all heavenly monotheistic religions: "Lo! this your religion is one religion, and I am your Lord, so worship Me."[10]

The Prophet wanted to mobilise under the orders of Allah all the believers in the holy books, including his own nation, to face polytheism and idolatry. However, the majority refused to believe him and opposed him.

Today, great nations have been established on the basis of denial of God and atheism. Their propaganda is raging in many countries. That is why the followers of heavenly religions should unite to defend their ideals in religion and life, before they become engulfed by such propaganda.

In such a serious situation, all should go back to sincere faith in One God as in the religion of Abraham. They should free their intellectual and religious life from all kinds of superstition and straighten their faith in One God on the basis of reason, just as Abraham did.

Question: Is there direct communication between God and Man?

Answer: Yes, communication does exist between God and man, according to the Qur'ān. "And certainly We created man, and We know what his mind suggests to him, and We are nearer to him than his life-vein."[11] It also explains: "And when those who worship Me ask thee concerning Me, surely I am nigh. I answer the prayer of the suppliant when he calls on Me."[12]

Islam finds no need for a mediator between God and man, be it priest, saint or pontiff. Every Muslim should know his religion properly and fully. He must not overlook the fact that he can get in contact with God at any time and in any place. He should know that between him and His Lord lies an area unknown even to the angels, who are supposed to know man's actions. The area is represented by man's conscience, which cannot be fathomed except by God.

It is true that there is a difference between Muslims who are well versed in religious matters and those of simple learning. It is the duty of the latter to learn from the former. But when a Muslim seeks help from a learned man, he realises that what he is seeking is contact with God, and that there is no need for a mediator to exist between them.

Question: Is God's guidance to Man a practical reality?
Answer: There is no doubt about that. It is certain that God is most Merciful and that He wants goodness for His creatures. "Never would God make your faith to be fruitless."[13] "Those who strive hard for Us, we shall certainly guide them in Our ways."[14]

The Prophet Muḥammad used to say, "God is more merciful to His servants than a mother to her son." It is God who has guided man over the centuries. When the first man disobeyed His order, He sent him down to earth, but still with His guidance. When man erred, "Then Adam received words from his Lord, and He turned to him mercifully."[15] "There will surely come to you guidance from Me: then whoever follows My guidance, he will not go astray nor be unhappy. And whoever turns from My Message, for him surely there is a strained life."[16]

When man reached intellectual maturity, God sent him His last Book, which is the permanent light, and guidance: the Holy Qur'ān.

God's guidance to man is also manifest in granting him intellect to discover through the sciences the secrets of nature. He made nature subservient to man. It is impossible to believe that man has gone up to conquer space and split the atom without God's guidance.

Present and future discoveries are confirmation of man's position in the universe, which was previously explained by all the prophets through Divine revelation. Modern science indicates God's help and guidance to man in this life. Without this help, nature would have remained a secret. It was God's religion that guided man in days of ignorance. It was the knowledge God enabled man's mind to grasp that led him to enlightenment and power.

Science should urge man to worship God with logic and reason, while religion drives man to worship Him with heart and soul.

# Supplement II

## Universal Islamic Declaration of Human Rights

The Fifteenth Century of the Islamic era opened on 9 November 1980 AD, (1 Muharram 1401 AH). The year before and the year following this date were a period of intense activity throughout the Muslim world. Behind the turbulent political conflicts of the time Muslim scholars, writers and economists, as well as many of the rank and file of practising Muslims in different walks of life, were seeking to deepen their understanding of their faith. It was an opportunity, said Dr Inamullah Khan, Secretary General of the World Muslim Congress, "to take stock of the gains and losses of the Muslims in the 1400 years. We should not only talk about our achievements but also our failures and the pitfalls into which we have been falling . . . As Islam wants to build an egalitarian and a humanitarian society the two-year Hijra celebration should be for correcting past mistakes in all fields of life, be it educational, cultural, social, not ignoring the very important part that economics play in modern life today."[1]

To bring an eternal message to the attention of mankind involves a continuing battle to clarify its meaning and to purify its expression, in the lives and in the statements of Muslim believers. Two such statements were issued by the Islamic Council of Europe: the *Universal Islamic Declaration*, April 1980, which stressed that "a universal order can be created only on the basis of a universal faith and not by serving the gods of race, colour, territory or wealth";[2] followed by the *Universal Islamic Declaration of Human Rights*, September 1981, "based on the Qur'ān and the Sunnah and compiled by eminent Muslim scholars, jurists and representatives of Islamic movements and thought."

The Declaration follows the lines of the Declaration of Human Rights, issued in 1948 by the General Assembly of the United Nations. It has 23 clauses:—the Right to Life, to Freedom, to Equality, to Justice, to Fair Trial etc. There is a basic difference of approach. The United Nations Declaration starts with "the recognition of the inherent dignity and of the equal and inalienable rights of all members of the human family." The Muslim Declaration looks to "the Divine source and sanction of these rights." "We, as Muslims, believe . . . that each one of us is under a bounden duty to spread the teachings of Islam by word and deed, and indeed in all gentle ways, and to make them effective not only in our individual lives but also in the society around us."

The Rights of Minorities are included. "The Qur'ānic principle, 'There is no compulsion in religion', shall govern the religious rights of non-Muslim minorities." The "Right to found a family" (common to both Declarations) is followed by a section on the rights of married women. Explanatory notes point out that throughout the Declaration "person" refers to both the male and female sexes: and also that each of the Rights expressed carries a corresponding duty.

"This is a declaration for mankind, a guidance and instruction to those who fear God."

Qur'ān: Sūra 3: 138 Al-'Imrān[3]

## A Note on the Illustrations

The oneness of God and the essential unity of His creation are basic to Islamic art, as they are to all Muslim life and thought. This is reflected in an exactness of mathematical design which gives serenity in architecture and undergirds all the arts.

Light is one: yet when broken by a prism it reveals every shade of colour. The millions of mankind are all equal – all sons of Adam, made of clay – yet in that equality there is scope for the differences of human personality, and never in all history have two individuals been identical. So it is with design: mathematically perfect, yet infinitely varied.

This perfection of pattern is given life in different ways: by the flowing lines of the Arabic script, drawn with the master skill of the calligraphers; by the floral designs that recall the "gardens through which rivers flow" so often described in the Qur'ān; by the reshaping of triangle, square, and circle swept, as it were, by the movement of wind or water.

Through the illustrations given in this book may be perceived something of this interweaving of the absolute and the infinite, the abstract and the actual, form and life. The pictures are drawn from many sources, ranging from the early splendours of the thirteen-centuries-old Dome of the Rock to the London Central Mosque of 1976.

# Postscript to Second Edition

Much has happened since this book was first published. The wide-spread resurgence of Islam has developed in many forms. The coming of a new Muslim century has been the occasion of broad publicity and deep thought. World events have focussed attention on one aspect of the Muslim world after another.

Some of the voices that spoke so clearly then have been stilled: among them that great-hearted scholar Dr Abdul Halim Mahmud, whose words appear on the title page; and Sayyida Faṭima al-Yashru-ṭiyya, whose quiet faith was a light far beyond the mountains of Lebanon where she died. It is both humbling and heartening to find, in her last book published after her death, an appreciation of *The Muslim Mind*.[1]

Other voices have been raised, particularly in the sphere of relations between men of different faiths – and notably between Christians and Muslims. In November 1979, Pope John Paul II visited Turkey and made his journey an occasion for speaking about Islam, and about its followers "who hold like us the faith of Abraham in the One Almighty and Merciful God." "When I think of this spiritual heritage and the value it has for man and society, I ask myself if it is not urgent, today as Christians and Muslims have entered a new period of history, to recognise and develop the spiritual bonds that unite us."[2] This, he continues, must be done "in order to preserve and promote together for the benefit of all men, peace, liberty, social justice and moral values." This is more than dialogue replacing polemic. Common ground is envisaged as the basis for common action in the service of mankind.

Not long after this, a respected Muslim leader – looked to by millions of his people for spiritual as well as political leadership – crossed the Channel to Dover. He said to his wife, "Now is the time to visit Canterbury." "Our visit to the Cathedral next morning," he told me, "coincided with a service commemorating the Battle of Britain, forty years ago. From all over the country ex-airmen came. Some were disabled, some even had to be carried in. There was a wonderful atmosphere and for me it was a very spiritual hour."

On the way out he noticed more than one memorial tablet speaking of officers who died fighting in Muslim lands. He was saddened to recall how much of Britain's history has been bound up in violent clash with Arab, African and Asian peoples, struggles in which his own family have fought and suffered much, for he is a grandson of the great Sayed Muhammad al-Mahdi of the Sudan.

"In my opinion," said Sayed Ahmed El-Mahdi, "the peace and future of the whole world depend on whether Muslims and Christians can pool the resources of our great faiths, learn to listen to and respect each other, and find a common strategy in the face of militant materialism." Appealing for a Christian response, he added, "A simple thought came to me the other day. The conflict between Christians and Muslims led us nowhere, so perhaps it was not what God wanted. Perhaps it is God's will that we now try different patterns of response to each other."[3]

It was to Canterbury in 597 AD that the great Pope Gregory sent St Augustine to take the message of Christianity to England. They were contemporaries of the Prophet Muḥammad. The conversion of the Arabs to Islam, and of the Angles to Christianity, were both to have profound effects in history.

Centuries later, in 1076 AD, a few years before the First Crusade, another Pope Gregory was to write to a Muslim ruler in North Africa, "We believe in and confess One God, the Creator of the worlds and the Ruler of this world."[4] This clear echo of the opening verses of the Qur'ān, the *Fātiḥa*, marked a moment of hope – and of choice. History took a different course, and the memory of the Crusades still embitters Muslim-Christian relations. St Francis struck a different note, but it was not until our own times that a Pope would thus again speak words of brotherhood to Muslims.

This book was designed to give a platform to Muslims to speak their minds. But I may perhaps be allowed a personal word. *The Muslim Mind* was conceived as a response to the situation following the Six-Day War of June 1967. I myself left East Jerusalem in late May. In the months that followed, relationships between Britain and the Arab world – and wider afield in the Muslim world – were at a low ebb. A yawning gulf of misunderstanding and ignorance seemed to have sundered the links of friendship. The gap in the western mind with regard to Islam, caused by historical circumstances and by a neglect of the whole subject in our education system, had become a serious obstacle to any intelligent approach to the tangle of injustices in the Middle East – a tangle which our own policies had done much to produce.

To one who had grown up amid the hopes and fears of the Palestine of the 1920's and 1930's the burden of that responsibility was a real one. I was brought up in Palestine, and in those childhood years I began to learn a vital lesson in human relations: to respect what other people believe, while being loyal to one's own deepest convictions. My father – who brought his Australian family to live in Jerusalem in 1919, and whose educational work brought him into touch with all the varied communities in that unique city – was ahead of his time in his vision of a new co-operation. He spoke to Christian, Muslim and Jew alike of "the comradeship of our joint belief" in One God, so much more important than all that divides us. And he called for "the energetic diffusion of the spirit that is the opposite of antagonism."[5]

Returning to the Middle East in the 1960's, one thing I learned was that both sides felt themselves betrayed by our self-interested policies. The serious imbalance of information was of no help to anyone, Jew or Arab. But it was not the facts of a case that were most needed. It was something deeper, which could lay the foundations of a new structure of relationships in an area where the old ones were in ruins.

I found myself trying to deal with the caricatures of the Muslim and the Arab, so deeply engraved in the western mind. Few cared to ask what Islam looked like to those who actually believed and practised it. Yet this was a question which I was equipped to ask.

And so, encouraged by many Muslim friends, I offered a platform on which Muslims could express what they themselves wanted to say about their own beliefs. It was not lightly done, and it took me nine years. When I had finished the book the situation was already very different. World events had opened many people's eyes and there was a growing acknowledgment of the general ignorance concerning the Muslim world, and also – amid the many reactions to the oil crisis and other developments – a genuine desire to learn. Books were beginning to pour out, but there was still little that could lay the foundations of a sympathetic understanding of a creed and code of behaviour underlying the faith and practice of nearly a quarter of mankind.

Today the Muslim world is in a far stronger position, and the state of public opinion in the West vastly different. In most western lands, the Muslim is a responsible fellow citizen, no longer a stranger, and mosques are a familiar feature of many cities. While there is still much need for information and education – and this must become a permanent in-built feature of our life – the frontier can move on to new areas of co-operation.

Little change has been made in this edition. The turbulent events of the past years have underlined, not altered, the importance of the truths voiced in these pages. Two further words may be added, enriching the quality of life which a believer can carry into the tasks that face him.

The extent of God's leading in the life of a man is one of the biggest and most profound questions in any age, not least our own. Islam distinguishes clearly between the *revelation* (*waḥy*) of truth which God gave only to the prophets: and the *guidance* in the Straight Path (*hudā*) which every believer prays for many times a day. Dr Fadhel Jamali, speaking about this out of a lifetime's experience in public as well as private life, quoted two verses of the Qur'ān. "God will not change the condition of a people, until that people change what is in themselves." "God guides those He wills: and he knows best those who receive guidance."[6] Christians can also learn from this honest searching of heart, combined with an absence of judgment.

A similar cleansing honesty runs through Dr Abdel Halim Mahmud's last book, *The Creed of Islam*. He quotes this Saying: "My servants, you make mistakes by day and night, and I forgive all sins: ask My forgiveness and I will forgive you." He adds, "The first brick in the palace of sincerity and the first tree to be planted in its garden is repentance, total and sincere repentance." And he gathers together some of the teaching in the Qur'ān and the traditions of the Prophet about God's forgiveness. "Do not despair of God's mercy, for He forgives all sins: He is the Forgiving One, the Merciful." Together with the warning. "Is there not in hell a home for the arrogant?"[7]

Every generation in turn faces its own crisis of choice between materialism and faith. The biggest ideological question facing humanity today is whether or not the forces of faith will decide to work together to meet the urgent needs of mankind.

It is to offer some small contribution to this momentous choice that this edition of *The Muslim Mind* is presented.

# Notes

## INTRODUCTION (page xv-xx)

1   *News of Muslims in Europe* No. 12, 27/1/82, Centre for the Study of Islam and Christian-Muslim Relations, Birmingham, U.K., quoting a Research Paper containing "the results of the latest attempt to estimate the size of the Muslim population of the continent of Europe". See also M. Ali Kettani, *Muslim Minorities in the World Today*, Institute of Muslim Minority Affairs and Mansell Publishing Ltd, London 1986, *Muslims in Europe*, pp. 21–53

2   *World Muslim Gazetteer*, 1985, ed. Inamullah Khan, Mo'tamar al-Alam al-Islami (World Muslim Congress), Umma Publishing House, Karachi, p. 10.

3   *Arabia* (Islamic World Review) September 1981, No. 1, summarises the history of *China's Muslim Millions*. Population estimates, p. 39. A Chinese Muslim who has written in English on the subject is Hajji Ibrahim T.Y. Ma, diplomat and scholar. He quotes fourteen modern works in Chinese as his sources. *The Muslims in China* Noor al-Islam, Utusan Melayu Berhad, Kuala Lumpur 1975. See also Kettani op. cit. pp. 82–106

4   *A Godly Consultation unto the Brethren and the Companyons of the Christian Religion, Theodor Bibliander being the author*, printed at Basel, 1542, in Latin and English editions; Bodleian Library

5   Dr A. I. Othman, interview, January 1969

6   Dr Hassan Hathout, letter, 1968

## CHAPTER ONE (pages 2–10)

1   *Bulletin of Christian Institutes of Islamic Studies*, Hyderabad, July-October 1971, p. 14; by permission of Muslim Educational Association of Southern India

2   Maulana Abul Kalam Azad *Tarjuman al-Qur'ān*, Vol. I, *Sūrat al-Fātiḥa*, edited by Syed Abdul-Latif, Asia Publishing House, Bombay, 1962, p. 193

3   M. El-Zayyat *Questions to a Moslem: An Exposition*, Egyptian Embassy, Washington, 1954, p. 7

4   A. M. Said Salama *Islam, A Progressive Faith for a Dynamic World*, Al Karnak, Cairo, pp. 75–7

5 Interview, 1970
6 Mrs Fareeza Taji, conversation, April 1973
7 *Al-Rātib*; printed by permission of Abderrahman al Mahdi, Cairo, 1957, pp. 41, 125
8 Qur'ān: Sūra 2: 185 *The Cow*
9 Dr Sayed Mushtaq Husein *Zakāt*, Islamic Correspondence Course, Unit 6, Minaret House, London

## CHAPTER TWO (pages 11–18)

1 Mediaeval philosopher; see p. 172
2 Interview, 16 January 1969
3 United Nations Relief and Works Association, the United Nations body responsible for the care and education of the Palestinian refugees
4 Interview, December 1968, and A. I. Othman *Concept of Man in Islam in the writings of Al-Ghazāli*, Dar el Maaref, Cairo 1960, pp. 15, 13
5 Sayyid Abul A'lā Mawdūdī *Towards Understanding the Qur'ān*, English version of *Tafhīm al-Qur'ān*, trans. and ed. by Z. I. Ansari, Islamic Foundation, Leicester vol. I 1988, vol. II 1989.
6 Altaf Gauhar *Translations from the Qur'ān*, Islamic Information Services, London, UK Edition 1977 (First published 1975) pp. 1, 47–8, 50, 54
7 Abdullah Yusuf Ali *The Holy Qur'ān: Text, Translation and Commentary*, Dar al Arabia, Beirut, 1965, Vol. I, p. 312, notes 903–6

## CHAPTER THREE (pages 19–32)

1 Ahmad Kamal *The Sacred Journey*, Allen and Unwin, London, 1964, p. 32
2 *Aramco World*, Vol. 32, No. 4, July-August 1981, p. 9. Pilgrimage Statistics 1974/1394, Ministry of the Interior, Saudi Arabian Government
3 The cube-shaped building in the centre of the Sacred Precinct, Mecca. The Arabic word *ka'b* means "cube".
4 *Pilgrimage Hajj*, Unit 5, Islamic Correspondence Course, Minaret House, London, pp. 3–5
5 A. Abdul Hameed, "Reflections on Ḥajj 1968", *The Muslim*, January 1969, pp. 77–80
6 H. Hathout *Ḥajj, Pilgrimage, Form and Essence*, Kuwait 1972, pp. 58–9

7 Large crowds in India were still addressed in this way until the use of microphones became general.
8 Sayed Muzaffar-ud-din Nadvi *An Easy History of the Prophet of Islam*, Lahore, 1954, reprinted 1963, pp. 131–2

## CHAPTER FOUR (pages 34–44)

1 Special Paper 1969
2 Qur'ān: Sūra 2: 283 *The Cow*
3 Qur'ān: Sūra 2: 150 *The Cow*
4 Qur'ān: Sūra 4: 36 *Women*
5 Qur'ān: Sūra 5: 54 *The Table*
6 Qur'ān: Sūra 2: 186 *The Cow*
7 Qur'ān: Sūra 2: 256 *The Cow*
8 Qur'ān: Sūra 49: 13 *The Apartments*
9 Qur'ān: Sūra 2: 136 *The Cow*
10 Qur'ān: Sūra 2: 284 *The Cow*
11 Qur'ān: Sūra 24: 33 *Light*
12 For *Zakāt* see p. 10

## CHAPTER FIVE (pages 45–55)

1 Abdel Moghny Said, *Arab Socialism*, Blandford Press, 1972, p. 24
2 Muhammad Qutb, "Islam and the Crisis of the Modern World", in *Islam, Its Meaning and Message*, ed. Khurshid Ahmad, Islamic Council of Europe, 1975, p. 256
3 M. U. Chapra, "Objectives of the Islamic Economic Order", in *Islam, Its Meaning and Message*, op. cit. pp. 178–9 (abridged)
4 Abdel Moghny Said *Arab Socialism*, Blandford Press, 1972, pp. 24–5
5 Rami G. Khouri, "Islamic Banking", *Aramco World Magazine*, May/June 1987, p. 18
6 Ed. Muazzam Ali *Islamic Banks and Strategies of Economic Cooperation*, published for the International Association of Islamic Banks by New Century Publishers, London, 1982, pp. 10–11, 20–21
7 Quoted by Sayyid Abul-Hasan Ali Nadwi *Western Civilisation – Islam and Muslims*, trans. from Urdu by Dr M. A. Kidwai, Academy of Islamic Research, Lucknow, English edition, 1979, p. 200
8 S. H. Nasr, seminar on *Islamic Thought – A Living Tradition*, Oxford Centre for Islamic Studies, 26/2/1988
9 A. R. I. Doi, "Re-Islamisation of the West African Ummah: A Model for Tajdīd?", *American Journal of Islamic Social Sciences*, Vol. 4, No. 2, 1987

10 Mervyn Heskitt *The Sword of Truth, The Life and Times of the Shehu Usuman Dan Fodio*, OUP, New York, 1973, p. 121. Muhammad Ali *The Religion of Islam*, Lahore, 1950, p. 263

11 *New Horizons for Africa* (leaflet) and personal reports.

12 Nadwi, op. cit., pp. 3, 4, 13–14, 33


## CHAPTER SIX (pages 56–74)

1 K. Ahmad *Family Life in Islam*, The Islamic Foundation, Leicester, 1974, p. 13

2 A. M. Said *Arab Socialism*, pp. 122–3

3 K. Ahmad, op. cit., p. 19

4 ibid., p. 32. In a review of *Family Life in Islam*, Clifford Longley, Religious Affairs Correspondent of *The Times*, comments (23 December 1974): "Though so-called Christian family life is under intolerable strain, Islamic family life appears better designed to stand up to contemporary pressures . . . Mr Ahmad's belief that the preservation of family life is essential for the welfare and prosperity of nations is one that many Christians and Jews would share, and many humanists. If so, the Islamic nations may be in a strong position in the world today not just because of Arab oil wealth but because they possess a stable system of domestic relationships such as the West is trying to do without."

5 K. Ahmad, op. cit., pp. 21–2

6 Interview, March 1966

7 M. Smith, *Rābi'a the Mystic*, Cambridge 1928, p. 27. M. Paul, *Loving God for Himself Alone, An Appreciation of the prayers of a Muslim Mystic, Rābi'a of Basrah*, SLG Press, Oxford, 1975, p. 7. See C. Waddy, *Women in Muslim History*, Longman 1980, Chapter 5 passim

8 *Women in Muslim History*, pp. 40–47, N. Abbott, *Two Queens of Baghdad*, Chicago 1946. For recent archaeological research along the pilgrim road which Zubaida so much improved, see Dr Saad A. Al-Rashid, *Darb Zubaydah, The Pilgrim Road from Kufa to Mecca*, Riyad, 1980

9 C. Waddy, *New Opportunities for Jordan's Women*, Middle East International, July 1977, pp. 29–31

10 Sayid M. M. Lari, *Western Civilisation through Muslim Eyes*, English translation by F. J. Goulding, 1977. Orders through Optimus Books, Montague Place, Worthing, Sussex BN11 3BG, or the author, Entezam St. 21, Qum, Iran

11 A. Yusuf Ali, *The Holy Qur'ān, Text Translation and Commentary*, Beirut 1965, pp. 904, 1126

12 Mme Nouha Alhegelan, *Women in the Arab World, Irish Arab News*, Summer 1978, p. 12
13 Letter from Mrs Taraneh Azima-Kayhan, May 1979. See also pp. 136–7
14 S. H. Nasr *Ideals and Realities*, Allen and Unwin, 1966, pp. 70–1
15 Qur'ān: Sūra 4: 1, 3 *Women*
16 S. H. Tabandeh *A Muslim Commentary on the Declaration of Human Rights*, London, 1970, translated by F. J. Goulding, pp. 62–6 (summarised)
17 A. A. A. Fyzee *Outlines of Muhammadan Law*, Third Edition, Oxford University Press, 1964, pp. 85–6, 118
18 A. M. Said *Islam – A Progressive Faith for a Dynamic World*, Cairo, p. 74
19 Quoted in "Focus on Population", Special Number of *Mid-East, A Middle East-North African Review*, September/October 1968, p. 5
20 ibid., p. 22
21 Yusuf Al-Qaradawi *The Lawful and the Prohibited in Islam*, Shorouk International, London 1985, pp. 198, 201
22 op. cit., pp. 201–2
23 See also *Journal of the Kuwait Medical Association*, I: 95, 1967

## CHAPTER SEVEN (pages 75–81)

1 A. Yusuf Ali *The Holy Qur'ān: Text, Translation and Commentary*, notes 3430, 3431 (on Sūra 29: 8), and 3597–9 (on Sūra 31: 14–15), Vol. II, pp. 1030, 1083
2 Discussion with members of the Muslim Women's Association, London, June 1968

## CHAPTER EIGHT (pages 84–98)

1 Lawyer and writer, Beirut, Interview, 1968
2 A. Wessels *A Modern Arabic Biography of Muhammad: A Critical Study of Muhammad Husayn Haykal's Ḥayat Muḥammad*, Leiden, Brill, 1972, p. 151
3 A. Yusuf Ali, op. cit., note 10
4 ibid., note 4586
5 ibid., note 754
6 Dr Ali Issa Othman, Interview, January 1969
7 Asia Plateau, Moral Re-Armament Conference Centre, completed 1973
8 Miss Neerja Choudhury *Himmat*, 4 February 1972

9 Interview, 1968
10 December 1968
11 The army coup which overthrew the government of Menderes and Bayar
12 *Milliyet*, Istanbul, 31 December 1972, cf. A. E. Yalman *Turkey in My Time*, Oklahoma Press, 1956


# CHAPTER NINE (pages 99–111)

1 Quoted by M. Khadduri *Arab Contemporaries*, Johns Hopkins Press, 1973, p. 108
2 Article in *L'Express*, 5 February 1955
3 M. H. Haykal in A. Wessels, op. cit., pp. 232–3
4 Interview 1968
5 Quoted by A. Duncan *The Noble Sanctuary*, Longman, 1972, p. 22
6 Interview, January 1969
7 Interview, 1969
8 A. Yusuf Ali, op. cit., note 1270, Vol. I, p. 444
9 Maulana Abul Kalam Azad *Tarjumān al-Qur'ān*, Vol. I, Bombay, 1962, pp. xlii-xliii
10 *The Times*, 19 July 1961
11 Joseph P. Lash *Dag Hammarskjold*, Cassell, London, 1962, p. 124
12 Brian Urquhart *Hammarskjold*, Bodley Head, London, p. 290
13 ibid., p. 293
14 M. A. Mahgoub *Democracy on Trial*, André Deutsch, 1974, pp. 95–9
15 *Mideast Mirror*, Beirut, 24 August 1958
16 Rajmohan Gandhi, September 1958. Grandson of Mahatma Gandhi; was Editor-in-chief of the Bombay weekly *Himmat*
17 Message to World Assembly for Moral Re-Armament, Caux, Switzerland, 1966. See also F. N. D. Buchman *Remaking the World*, Blandford, London, 1961, pp. 224, 252–3, G. D. Lean, *Frank Buchman; a life*, Constable 1985, pp. 507–8
18 Memorandum, 1969. See further, Supplement I, pp. 189–196


# CHAPTER TEN (pages 112–118)

1 A. J. Toynbee *Civilisation on Trial*, Oxford University Press, 1948, pp. 205–6
2 'Abd al-Rahmān 'Azzām *The Eternal Message of Muḥammad*, Devin Adair, New York, 1964; Mentor Paperback, New York, 1965, p. xx
3 ibid., pp. 218–21

4 Qur'ān: Sūra 109: 6 *Disbelievers*
5 Qur'ān: Sūra 2: 256 *The Cow*
6 Qur'ān: Sūra 10: 100 *Jonah*
7 Interview, April 1972
8 *The Autobiography of Malcolm X*, with the assistance of Alex Haley, Hutchinson of London, 1965, pp. 411–13, 418–20, 460
9 K. Cragg *Alive to God*, Oxford University Press, 1970, p. 54
10 E. Cleaver *Soul on Ice*, London, 1969, p. 66
11 From a review of *The Autobiography of Malcolm X* (first published in the USA in 1965, Penguin Edition 1968) by M. A. Sherif, *The Muslim*, London, October 1968


## CHAPTER ELEVEN (pages 119–128)

1 Interview, February 1972
2 Late Imam of the Islamic Cultural Centre, London. Interview, 15 July 1968
3 *Majallat al-Azhar*, March 1959, pp. 789–91, quoted in MIDEO (*Mélanges de l'Institut Dominicain d'Études Orientales*), Vol. 5, pp. 436–7, 1959
4 Qur'ān: Sūra 2: 257 *The Cow*
5 Qur'ān: Sūra 5: 85 *The Table*
6 S. Mahmassani *The Principles of International Law in the Light of Islamic Doctrine*, Academy of International Law, Recueil des Cours, Leiden, Vol. I, 1966, pp. 322–3
7 A. A. A. Fyzee *A Modern Approach to Islam*, Asia Publishing House, Bombay, 1963, p. 35
8 R. El-Droubie *Islam*, Ward Lock Educational, London, pp. 27–8
9 Conversation, December 1971
10 Conversation, 1972
11 Interview, 1968
12 Conversation, September 1968
13 Count Gérard d'Hauteville and F. J. Goulding, 1953
14 M. K. Hussein, *City of Wrong, a Friday in Jerusalem*, translated by K. Cragg, Bles, London, 1959, p. 67
15 ibid., p. 68
16 ibid., pp. 3–4


## CHAPTER TWELVE (pages 129–132)

1 Al-Ghazāli *Iḥyā al-'Ulūm*, iii. 149.11, quoted by A. Guillaume *The Traditions of Islam*, Oxford, 1924, p. 149

2 A. J. Arberry *Shiraz*, Oklahoma Press, 1960, p. 161
3 A. Azzam *Eternal Message of Muḥammad*, p. 32
4 Qur'ān: Sūra 56: 19 *The Event*
5 Qur'ān: Sūra 13: 23 *Thunder*
6 James Michener *Islam, the Misunderstood Religion*, reprinted *Reader's Digest*, May 1955, p. 4
7 Ahmad Kamal *The Sacred Journey*, Allen and Unwin, 1964, pp. 76, 80
8 *The Times*, 15 March 1974, and *The Guardian*, 16 March 1974, from *Yediot Ahranot*, Tel Aviv, and *Al Mussawar*, Cairo

## CHAPTER THIRTEEN (pages 133–137)

1 Mamdouh Mandour, medical student, President of the Cairo University Student Union: Report, British-Arab University Association, Visits, 1973
2 Naguia Said, School of Architecture, Cairo University, ibid.
3 Reports on visits arranged by the British-Arab University Association, 1973 onwards
4 Conversations, October 1972
5 Letters, 1972–73

## CHAPTER FOURTEEN (pages 140–144)

1 M. F. Jamali *Towards a Unity of Educational Thought in the Islamic World*, Tunis, 1972 (Arabic), p. 17
2 I. Shah *Pleasantries of the Incredible Mulla Nasruddin*, Cape, 1968, p. 133
3 *Letters on Islam, written by a father in prison to his son*, translated from the Arabic by the author, Mohammad Fadhel Jamali, World of Islam Festival Trust, London, 1978
4 *Tarbiyat al-insān al-jadīd*, Tunis, 1967
5 *'Āfāq it-tarbiyat il-ḥadītha fil-bilād in-nāmiya*, Tunis, 1968
6 *Nahwa tauḥīd il-fikr it-tarbawīyi fil-'ālam il-islāmīyi*, Tunis, 1972
7 "Man of the Future Seen through Eastern eyes", translated by C. W. in *The Times Educational Supplement*, 26 September 1968
8 Translated by C. W. in a review in *Middle East Forum*, Beirut, 1968, Vol. xiv, No. 3
9 Translated by C. W. from the Introduction

## CHAPTER FIFTEEN (pages 145–154)

1 M. Wahby *Arab Quest for Peace*, Orient Longman, Bombay, 1971, pp. 191, 193
2 *Echo*, World Confederation of Organisations of the Teaching Profession, February 1975
3 M. Y. McDermott, M. M. Ahsan *The Muslim Guide, For Teachers, Employers, Community Workers and Social Administrators in Britain*, Islamic Foundation, Leicester 1980, p. 89
4 Professor Kamel Tarzi, Union Tunisienne d'aide aux insuffisants mentaux, at the Congress of the International League of National Associations for Aid to the Mentally Handicapped, Vienna, 1978, paper entitled "The attitude of Islam concerning the integration of the mentally retarded into community life."
5 From the Preamble to the new constitution of Al-Azhar, published in *Majallat al-Azhar*, July 1961; issued by the Minister of State in charge of the affairs of Al-Azhar, H. E. Kamal al din Mahmud Rif'at
6 See Koenig Visit, p. 122
7 Interview, 1969
8 Interview, 1969. Student numbers, *Statistical Year Book*, Govt of Egypt, 1980
9 Interview, 1969
10 Interview, 1971
11 M. A. Zaki Badawi, *Islam in Britain*, Ta Ha Publishers Ltd, London 1981
12 op. cit., p. 17
13 Hajji Riadh El-Droubie, *Times Educational Supplement*, 21/12/73
14 Ghulam Sarwar, *Education Reform Act, 1988, What Can Muslims Do?*, Muslim Education Trust, London, March 1989, pp. 8–9
15 E. Cox and J. M. Cairns, *Reforming Religious Education*, Bedford Way Series, Institute of Education, University of London, 1989, p. 96
16 Interview 4/2/88
17 *The Muslim College, Provisional Prospectus*, 20–22 Creffield Rd, London W5 3RP, 1987, p. 5
18 M. A. Z. Badawi, op. cit., pp. 12, 29

## CHAPTER SIXTEEN (pages 156–174)

1 Quoted by Seyyed Hossein Nasr *Sufi Essays*, Allen and Unwin, 1972, p. 34
2 F. Rahman *Islam*, Weidenfeld and Nicolson, 1966, p. 254
3 Interview, 16 January 1969
4 Seyyed Hossein Nasr, "Sufism and the Perennity of the Mystical

Quest", Charles Strong Memorial Lecture, 1970, *Milla wa-Milla*, No. 10, 1970, reprinted in *Sufi Essays*, Allen and Unwin, 1972, pp. 31–2, 37, 40

5 Interview, 16 January 1969

6 *A Muslim Commentary on the Universal Declaration of Human Rights*, by Shaikh Sultanhussein Tabandeh, translated by F. J. Goulding: first Persian edition, 1966, English translation, F. T. Goulding and Co., London, 1970, pp. vii, ix

7 Fāṭima al-Yashruṭiyya:
  *Riḥlat ilā-l-ḥaqq* (Arabic), Dar al-Kutub, Beirut, undated
  *Nafaḥāt al-ḥaqq* (Arabic), Dar al-Kutub, Beirut, 1372/1963
  *Mawāhib al-ḥaqq* (Arabic), Dar al-Kutub, Beirut, 1375/1966
  *Masīratī fī ṭarīq al-ḥaqq*, edited by Shaikh Ahmad al-Yashruti. Beirut 1981 (first impression, 8,000 copies)
  It is humbling and encouraging to find, in this book completed in the last days of her life, an appreciation of *The Muslim Mind* and an account of my visits to her in 1973.

8 Shaikh Abdurrazak Shah Biyabani *Glimpses of Reality*, Pune, 1960; second edition 1968, pp. 2, 3, 5, 32

9 M. Lings, *A Muslim Saint of the Twentieth Century*, Allen and Unwin, 1961, revised edition *A Sufi Saint of the Twentieth Century*, 1971, pp. 18–21

10 A. J. Arberry *Sufism*, Allen and Unwin, 1950, p. 80

11 A. I. Othman *The Concept of Man in Islam, in the Writings of Al-Ghazāli*, Cairo, 1960, p. 103

12 Qur'ān: Sūra 24: 35 *Light*

## CHAPTER SEVENTEEN (pages 176–188)

1 M. Abduh *The Theology of Unity*, translated by I. Musa'ad, K. Cragg; Allen and Unwin, 1966, p. 148

2 Ziauddin Sardar *The Future of Muslim Civilisation*, Croom Helm, London 1979, p. 231

3 Altaf Gauhar *Translations from the Qur'ān*, London 1977, p. 34

4 Sayyid A. H. A. Nadwi *Western Civilisation – Islam and Muslims*, Lucknow 1979, p. 204

5 Ali Abdul Halim Mahmoud *Al-da'wat al-islāmiyya da'wat 'ālamiyya*, Higher Council for Islamic affairs, Cairo, 1969; from the Introduction, translated by C.W.

6 *Rābitat al-'Ālam al-Islāmī: An Introduction*, Mecca, 1975

7 *World Muslim Gazetteer*, Karachi, 1985, pp. 709, 717

8 Published in *God and Man in Contemporary Islamic Thought*, ed. Charles Malik, Beirut, 1972

9 ibid., pp. 12–15

10 Seyyed Hossein Nasr *The Encounter of Man and Nature*, Allen and Unwin, 1968, p. 15
11 ibid., p. 106
12 id. *Science and Civilisation*, Harvard, 1968, p. 125
13 id. *The encounter of Man and Nature*, p. 94
14 ibid., pp. 135–6
15 ibid., pp. 168–9
16 M. A. Mahgoub *Democracy on Trial*, A. Deutsch, 1974, pp. 305–6
17 K. Ahmad *Islam – Its Meaning and Message*, Islamic Council of Europe, 1975, pp. 174–5, 179
18 Interview with G. K. Lean, *Yorkshire Post*, April 1974. On the question of oil the Chief Director of the United Nations Environment Programme, Mr Maurice Strong, said: "The Arab oil embargo shocked the industrial world into realising that it faces an impending energy crisis. But although the Arabs produced the shock, they did not produce the crisis. It dramatised to the world the central truth that we must do a much better job of managing and caring for the precious and limited resources of our Only One Earth." *World Environment Day Pressbook*, UNEP, Nairobi, 5 June 1974
19 A. Gauhar, op. cit., pp. 157, 158–9, 162–3, 167, 172–3
20 Qur'ān: Sūra 13: 11 *Thunder*
21 From an article in *Al Wahda*, Arabic daily, Asmara, April 1969, reprinted in M. A. Surur *Moral Re-Armament in the Modern World*, Alameya Press, Cairo, 1975

## SUPPLEMENT I (pages 189–196)

1 See section on War and Peace, pp. 107–111
2 Qur'ān: Sūra 9: 24 *Repentance*
3 Qur'ān: Sūra 3: 18 *Imran*
4 Qur'ān: Sūra 22: 39 *Pilgrimage*
5 Qur'ān: Sūra 2: 190 *The Cow*
6 Qur'ān: Sūra 2: 194 *The Cow*
7 Qur'ān: Sūra 2: 193 *The Cow*
8 Qur'ān: Sūra 68: 4 *The Pen*
9 Qur'ān: Sūra 4: 13 *Women*
10 Qur'ān: Sūra 21: 92 *Prophets*
11 Qur'ān: Sūra 50: 16 *Qaf*
12 Qur'ān: Sūra 2: 186 *The Cow*
13 Qur'ān: Sūra 2: 143 *The Cow*
14 Qur'ān: Sūra 29: 69 *The Spider*
15 Qur'ān: Sūra 2: 37 *The Cow*
16 Qur'ān: Sūra 20: 24 *Tā Hā*

## SUPPLEMENT II (pages 197–198)

1 *Morning News*, Karachi, reprinted *Muslim World* 22/12/79
2 Islamic Council of Europe, *Islam and Contemporary Society*, Longman Group, 1982, p. 257
3 *Universal Islamic Declaration of Human Rights*, published by Islamic Council of Europe, September 1981, *passim*


## POSTSCRIPT (pages 199–202)

1 Faṭima Al-Yashruṭiyya, *Masīratī fī ṭarīq al-ḥaqq* (My Journey in the Path of Truth), ed. shaikh Ahmad Al-Yashruti, Beirut 1981
2 *Osservatore Romano*, 3/12/79
3 *New World News*, 11/10/80
4 N. Daniel, *The Arabs and Mediaeval Europe*, Longman Group 1975, p. 251
5 E. Waddy, *Stacy Waddy, Cricket, Travel and the Church*, Sheldon Press, 1938, p. 179, *The Times* 31/12/77
6 Qur'ān: Sūra 13: 11 Thunder, Sūra 28: 56 The Narration. Abdullah Yusuf Ali (The Holy Qur'ān, Text, Translation and Commentary, Beirut 1965) comments on this latter verse (p. 108), "All whom we love do not necessarily share our views or beliefs. We must not judge. God will guide whom He pleases as He pleases. He alone knows the true inwardness of things."
7 Abdel Halim Mahmud, *The Creed of Islam*, trans. M. Abdel Halim, World of Islam Festival Trust 1978, pp. 60, 61

# Index